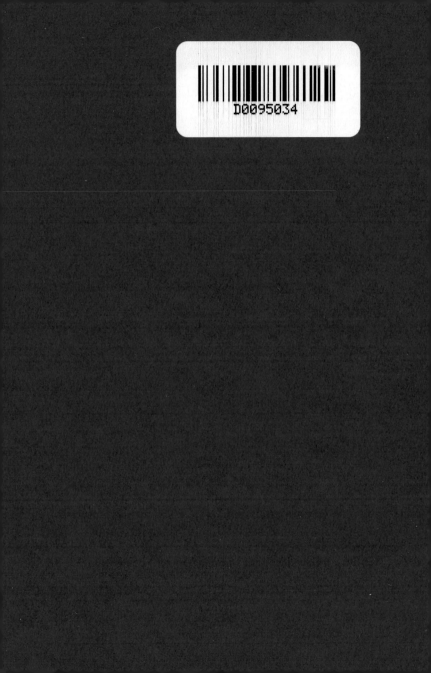

WRITING LESSONS
YOU CAN LEARN
FROM THE MASTER

write like

Hemingway

R. ANDREW WILSON, PhD

Aadamsmedia

AVON, MASSACHUSETTS

Published by
Adams Media, a division of F+W Media, Inc.
57 Littlefield Street, Avon, MA 02322. U.S.A.
www.adamsmedia.com

ISBN-10: 1-59869-896-6
ISBN-13: 978-1-59869-896-1

Printed in the United States of America.

J I H G F E D C B A

Library of Congress Cataloging-in-Publication Data
is available from the publisher.

This publication is designed to provide accurate and authoritative information with regard to the subject matter covered. It is sold with the understanding that the publisher is not engaged in rendering legal, accounting, or other
professional advice. If legal advice or other expert assistance is required,
the services of a competent professional person should be sought.
—From a *Declaration of Principles* jointly adopted by a Committee of the
American Bar Association and a Committee of Publishers and
Associations

Many of the designations used by manufacturers and sellers to distinguish
their product are claimed as trademarks. Where those designations appear
in this book and Adams Media was aware of a trademark claim, the designations have been printed with initial capital letters.

This book is available at quantity discounts for bulk purchases.
For information, please call 1-800-289-0963.

Dedication

For Jennifer

Acknowledgments

This book presumes that any act of writing is strongly influenced by both the people around an author and the models to whom he looks for guidance. I'm grateful first of all to Ernest Miller Hemingway. Without Papa's dedication to the writing craft and his inestimable talents, generations of writers would be lesser than they are. Jennifer Kushnier, my wife, encouraged me early on, critiqued a first draft, and offered thoughtful feedback throughout the writing process. The folks at Adams Media proved invaluable at making this book a reality—especially Paula Munier, who proposed the initial idea; Wendy Simard, my editor; Matthew Glazer; Richard Wallace, Colleen Cunnigham, and Michelle Kelly. Mitchell A. Smolow provided sound legal advice and is a good friend to have amidst a whitewater rapid. T. Kenneth Wilson was an early mentor who helped me appreciate the art of a Hemingway sentence.

Contents

Papa Hemingway, Writer of the World

Preface

"I can't think of any other in history who directly influenced so many writers. Especially young writers."

(John O'Hara on Hemingway's legacy, *New York Times*, 3 July 1961)

Sitting atop a peak in New Hampshire's Presidential Range shows you just how flawed human eyesight can be. From the mountain's base, its sides seem to ascend in elegant slabs. At the summit, however, you see the rocky shoulders for what they are: piles of stacked rubble. Each rock comes at blunted, odd points. Each boulder's skin is calloused, coarse. They hold the centuries of wear from White Mountain winters. Finding your balance is difficult. Sitting is uncomfortable.

I realize that I was seeing this mountainscape in the way that Ernest Hemingway taught me. Not as a grand, sweeping picture, but as piece built upon piece. Rock upon rock. Sensation upon sensation. I think of the opening of *For Whom the Bell Tolls*, Robert Jordan lying along a mountainside and watching the dark road that he's to block the Fascists from taking.

Looking out across a forested ravine, I see the Mount Washington Auto Road in the distance. Its black surface shines in the morning sunlight. Lone clouds had passed through earlier, sprinkling the ridges. The Auto Road isn't busy just yet, but by afternoon trains of tourists will follow it to the summit. They'll park their cars, get out, enjoy the view. Enjoy lunch. They'll come down with a bumper sticker.

That view is worth taking in. These sights are why I bother using a different route up. The climb by foot, backpack weighing on your shoulders, forces you to slow down. Unhurried by traffic, you take in each tree. Each rock. Each animal. It's the way one of Hemingway's sentences forces you to slow down. Take in the details. Hemingway may not have been on this peak, but his way of seeing the world has.

On my way back down that day, I'm near the end of the Six Husbands Trail. One of the steepest ways down from the summit, the trail is also one of the most direct routes up. Where the

trail levels off in the Great Gulf, I'm surprised by a woman standing in the middle of the path.

"How much further is the summit?" she asks.

I cock my head, unsure if she's joking. "Far enough."

She's with a bearded man. Both wear matching hip-packs.
Slung from their waists, each has a pair of plastic water bottles,
the kind you get free with a bicycle.

"Do you think we have time to make it up and back?"

The man pulls a handkerchief from his pack. He wipes it
across his brow.

"I don't know," I say. "It's kinda late in the day."

"The magazine said it could be done in a day."

"Well, we should've left earlier."

"And whose fault would that be?"

"Maybe we should stick to reading magazines."

Listening to their exchange, I'm not hearing this woman and
man so much as I'm hearing characters out of Hemingway. The
man and Jig in "Hills Like White Elephants," using idle chat
about alcohol and hills to stave off what they're trying to avoid
discussing. The husband and wife in "Out of Season," quarreling
over bad weather and fishing laws.

If Hemingway taught me something about how to see the
landscape, he also taught me something about how to see people.
And a fight over a drink that tastes like licorice or an ill-planned
hiking trip suggests much more than the surface tells.

The idea of this book is to learn what we can about writing
from Ernest Hemingway, the man who did more than any other
American author to change the face of the English written word.
He also changed the way we use literature to see the world that
we inhabit.

We're going to read Ernest Hemingway deliberately, both the stories that he created and the life that enabled his craft. We'll begin by following Hemingway over the years that he learned to write: the boy who started as a journeyman reporter, the teenager who went off to war but came back with experiences to put to ink, and the man whose matured writing style was manifest in *The Sun Also Rises*. From there, we'll look at the essential techniques of storytelling as "Papa" Hemingway used them: style and voice, character, dialogue, setting and description, and narration and point of view.

Write Like Hemingway is designed for both aspiring writers who are new to Papa and old-time aficionados. We'll cover both the basics of story writing and the special techniques that made Hemingway's style powerful enough to win him both a Pulitzer and a Nobel Prize.

To use this book, you'll want to have your copy of Hemingway's *Complete Short Stories* nearby, whether its pages are new or dog-eared. And if you're inspired to open Papa's novels along the way, by all means do so. In each chapter, you'll find writing exercises that are inspired either from Hemingway's stories or from the master's advice to writers just starting out. These exercises will help you along—if you're unhappy with an aspect of one, change it into something that will get you writing. You can learn a lot from watching a master of the craft at work, but in the end it's only through practice that any apprentice learns the art.

Let us see what Papa has to teach us.

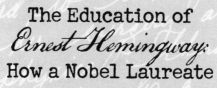

The Education of *Ernest Hemingway:* How a Nobel Laureate Learned to Write

1

"The hardest thing in the world to do is to write straight honest prose on human beings. First you have to know the subject; then you have to know how to write. Both take a lifetime to learn."

(Ernest Hemingway, "Old Newsman Writes: A Letter from Cuba"[1])

All writers, if they're any good, are asked at some point, "How did you do it?"

Ernest Hemingway was asked that question often during his life. In answering it, he could play the gate-keeping critic, pointing out the flaws in the literature of other writers, particularly those he sensed as competitors. But he could also enjoy playing the accomplished wordsmith to other writers. When he imagined F. Scott Fitzgerald's angered response to his criticisms of *Tender is the Night*, Hemingway exclaimed: "Jesus it's marvelous to tell other people how to write, live, die, etc."[2]

The popular image of Hemingway today is the fully formed "Papa." Robust and jowly, his face framed by a distinctive white beard, we picture him on safari in the African plains or on a boat riding the Atlantic waves. Rifle or rod in hand, he's ready to teach us to hunt, to fish. From Finca Vigía, his Cuban villa, he answers the phone to accept his Nobel Prize or corresponds with biographers chasing after his life's story. At Sloppy Joe's Bar, Papa's old haunt in Key West, the entrants for the annual Hemingway Look-Alike Contest invariably look like this elder statesman of storytelling, the man as he appeared in his fifties.

The nickname Hemingway preferred later in life, "Papa," certainly plays into this image. It's telling that Hemingway was going by that name while still in his twenties, as early as 1927.[3] He was then a father, and his first son, John, was known throughout childhood as "Bumby," a play on "baby." But he was also then the author of *The Sun Also Rises*, the novel that established him as a writer of international note. As his publishing success continued, the nickname "Papa" spread from family to friends. In Cuba, the baseball team he coached for his sons all took to calling him "Papa Hemingway."[4] So did younger writers who looked to him for advice. By the time of his death, anyone casually reciting the name "Papa" knew that it carried the legacy of the author from Illinois who changed how we thought about what literature could do.

Papa Says Hemingway allowed Marlene Deitrich to call him "Ernest," even though he preferred "Papa." Hemingway's nickname for Deitrich? "The Kraut."[5]

As this father figure of modernist literature, Hemingway has been praised for doing more to change the style of American writing than any other author. His stories tell us something startling and unique about the modern experiences of war and love, money and religion. But as a paternal authority he has been criticized for his shortcomings—too much machismo and often patently sexist, prejudiced, and anti-Semitic.

Pulling back the curtain on Papa's reputation, it's important to remember that he wasn't always such a literary force. Whatever literary genius Papa brought to his craft, it came after years of effort, revision, and learning from the writers around him. It's important also to remember the young Hemingway: the Hemingway who playfully went by "Hemingstein" as a teenager, who wrote tall tales back home that he was engaged to the film starlet Mae Marsh (whom he never met), or who first struggled to improve his writing and find a publisher.

Here, we'll trace the path of how Hemingway learned to write, from his early days as a junior newspaper reporter to the author that legendary editor Maxwell Perkins would take on at Charles Scribner's Sons. Perkins had brought a generation of younger writers to his company that included Hemingway, Fitzgerald, and Thomas Wolfe. Eager to publish the manuscript of *The Sun Also Rises*, Perkins explained to Hemingway that he was astonished by the novel's "extraordinary range of experience and emotion" that united in a "complete design."[6]

How did Papa learn to write such a novel?

The Newspaper Trade: Lessons in Kansas City

With a cub reporter's job waiting for him, Ernest Hemingway arrived in Kansas City at the age of eighteen to set about making his career as a writer.

In the spring, he had graduated from high school in Oak Park, Illinois, a middle-class suburb outside of Chicago. There, he published several fictional stories in the school's literary journal, typically at his English teachers' insistence. But the articles he also wrote for the school newspaper, *Trapeze,* provided the early experience for what became his first trade as a journalist. The subjects about which he wrote in the paper ranged from the debate club to the football team, and they often included satirical witticisms about his Oak Park High classmates. More than once, he published in the imitative style of Ring Lardner, occasionally adopting his name in the byline. The gesture was the sign of an aspiring writer, learning his craft, who styled himself after a fellow Midwesterner known for his *Saturday Evening Post* stories and Chicago journalism.

But in the fall of 1917 Hemingway was in Kansas City to make his own name as an author. With America's recent entry in the "Great War" and an eagerness for action, he might have joined the Army. His father, a successful physician, was against Hemingway going to war, and he had hopes that his son would continue a family tradition of attending Oberlin College. But Hemingway shirked his father's expectations. He spent the

summer of 1917 deciding upon his future. From June through
September, he worked hard on his family's Michigan farm and
fished rainbow trout out of Walloon Lake. For a time he contem-
plated leaving for California, enrolling at the University of Illinois, or taking on a job at the *Chicago Tribune*.

Seeing his son intent upon becoming a man of the typewriter—and wanting to delay as long as possible his becoming
a soldier of the trenches—Dr. Hemingway compromised with
Ernest's ambitions. The physician asked his brother, Alfred
Tyler Hemingway, to inquire about getting the youth a starting
position with the *Kansas City Star*.

Hemingway's Uncle Tyler was a successful businessman,
prospering in the lumber industry into which he had married.
He was also Oberlin classmates with Henry Haskell, who was
then the *Star's* top editorialist. After Tyler wrote to his old class-
mate, he found that his nephew could start as a reporter in the
fall. Hemingway arrived in Missouri on October 15, 1917, and
began his stint as a paid writer three days later, accompanied by
Tyler on his first-day's interview. As an apprentice newsman, he
earned $15 a week over the initial thirty days.

Decades later, Malcolm Cowley's flawed "A Portrait of Mister
Papa," appearing in *Life* magazine, would claim that Hemingway
had talked his own way into the *Kansas City Star* by misrepresent-
ing his age. By then, however, Cowley was caught in the myth of
Hemingway's self-determining machismo. His account was colored
by the aura of a sharp-talking youth, right out of high school, cutting out his own career as he would his distinctive writing style.

In reality, Hemingway relied upon the help of family and
friends more than once to advance his career and to find ways
of dedicating himself to his craft. In addition to Uncle Tyler's
help, Ralph Connable, a Canadian executive for Woolworth

stores, introduced him at the Toronto *Star*, which would publish more than twenty of Hemingway's pieces in its Saturday editions. Hemingway met Sherwood Anderson from Chicago's advertising circles, and the author of *Winesburg, Ohio* provided him with letters of introduction to the luminaries of Paris's Left Bank circle, among them Gertrude Stein and Ezra Pound. Once in France, supplementing his income as a correspondent for the Toronto *Star*, his first wife's modest trust fund supported the writer's socializing habits.

Hemingway Learns the Trade

In Kansas City, Hemingway was living apart from his family for the first time and learning the habits of a professional writer. His newspaper job provided him with two ingredients that flavored much of his future writing: a succinct style that would shape sentences around only the necessary, and a taste for the real-life violence, emotion, and anxiety of modern humanity.

Papa Says Hemingway in a letter from Cuba: "Your correspondent is an old newspaper man."[7]

At the *Star*, Hemingway reported to Clarence George Wellington, an editor nicknamed "Pete" who was known for his painstaking attention to style. Papa later remembered him as a strict but fair judge of a writer's work.[8] When Hemingway started at the paper, Wellington delivered to his desk the 110 commandments of the "*Star* Copy Style." The style sheet was meant to guide every sentence a reporter produced, every paragraph that fleshed out a story. Hemingway had the impression that a reporter must know these commandments, the standards by which all conduct would be judged, the way a soldier was meant to know the Articles of War.

As his fictional heroes would adopt a code of life and stick to it through war and failed romance, Hemingway's writing would always adhere to the principles he found at the *Star*. When Hemingway was interviewed in 1940—well after the success of *The Sun Also Rises* and *A Farewell to Arms*—he credited the *Star* style sheet as the "best rules" for prose he had known. In tones that cast good writing as the work of good manhood, Hemingway said: "No man with any talent, who feels and writes truly about the thing he is trying to say, can fail to write well if he abides with them."[9]

For today's writer, the 110 stylistic rules of the *Kansas City Star* offer such well-hewn suggestions as not to split infinitives and to keep verb tenses in order. In identifying the advice that marked Hemingway's voice as it later matured, however, biographers most frequently point to the sheet's opening dictums:

> *Use short sentences. Use short first paragraphs. Use vigorous English. Be positive, not negative.*

Short, short, vigorous, positive. Writing should give readers what the story is, directly, not what it might be or ought to be. The spirit of the *Star*'s copy sheet cut through the florid style expected in overly wrought literature. It reported plain Midwestern facts in a hard Midwestern voice.

The Oak Park High writer that Wellington inherited had a style, evident in his *Trapeze* bylines, modeled between flamboyance and ribaldry. Flaunting the lesson of alliteration—picked up, perhaps, from Pope—Hemingway lined up his "p" sounds in sentences such as the following: "A new party enters the race next fall in the person of the anti-prohibition party."[10] A party enters in the person of a party? The sentence was designed to show off a nascent poetic skill, with a delighted jab against Oak Park's temperance sensibilities. And when he experimented with the model found in Ring Lardner's "In the Wake of the News" columns, Hemingway adopted the punchy style of editorial satire.

A Newspaper Style "Avoid the use of adjectives, especially such extravagant ones as splendid, gorgeous, grand, magnificent, etc." —Rule 21 of the *Kansas City Star* Style Sheet.

The articles that Hemingway wrote in his six-and-a-half months at the *Star* show a style maturing into the serious and ironic detachment that would characterize some of his best-known works. And the short newspaper notices that Hemingway produced undoubtedly influenced the vignettes he published in his early collection, *In Our Time*, which he sold from Sylvia Beach's Parisian bookstore.

In one *Star* story, "Kerensky, The Fighting Flea" (1917), Hemingway described an office-boy pugilist: "In size, Leo is about right for a spanking. But that never will happen to Leo."[11] Boxing characters such as Leo would reappear with a frequency in Hemingway's fictional worlds—from Ad in "The Battler" to Ole in "The Killers" or Robert Cohen in *The Sun Also Rises*. The two sentences on Leo, nicknamed "Kerensky" due to his looking like the Russian revolutionary, also show the staccato rhythms of language that would come to typify the author's style. Together they form a chiasmus, a mirror-image reversal of sentence elements. "Leo" being ripe for a "spanking" but a "spanking" not ready for "Leo." The echoing of "Leo" from the first sentence's beginning against the close of the second showed the journeyman writer learning the ropes of a newspaper style's potential for poetry. Hemingway was practicing the ways in which the style of his writing could convey the weight of its substance.

"Mix War, Art, and Dancing" (April 21, 1918) was the article Hemingway reportedly liked best from these Kansas City days. On the surface the article was a news item about a soldiers' dance with the women of the Fine Arts Institute, but the story displays tones of Hemingway's budding literary talents. Hemingway describes the jazz-playing, fox-trotting crowd packed inside a YWCA as a counterpoint to a lone prostitute, walking the street outside. The story refers to this streetwalker three times, first in introducing the scene: "Outside a woman walked along the wet street-lamp lit sidewalk through the sleet and snow."[12] Continuing the writer's high-school experimentations with alliteration, the series of "w" and "s" sounds stamps the image of the prostitute into a reader's mind. Repeating the details of wet, sleet-driven sidewalk, Hemingway returns to her midway through his description of the dancers and then once more to conclude with her looking up at the darkened hall after the crowd has gone.

Hemingway recalled this *Star* story as "very sad, about a whore," not about the dance from which she was excluded.[13] The inclusion of the streetwalker, then, shows Hemingway's movement beyond the limitations of newspaper reportage into the more literary techniques of narrative framing and dramatic irony. As a reporting device, the detail about the hooker served little purpose in recounting the YWCA dance, except to set it amidst the city's underworld of petty crime or else to allude to what might otherwise occupy a waiting soldier's time. As a framing device, the prostitute served to establish a unity to the story that went beyond the lead writing typical of journalese, the expected standards of who, what, where, and when. As a literary device, though, the image captures a sense of irony, setting the camaraderie of the soldiers and their dancing partners against the loneliness of a solitary streetwalker. The article was the last Hemingway published before leaving for the Italian front of World War I.

A Dose of Life

As Hemingway was honing his writing style under Wellington's tutelage, his ambition also led him to seek out the grist of Kansas City's police stations and hospitals. Initially, Hemingway was assigned to cover the Federal Building during his first weeks as a trial reporter, but the young writer bristled for a more desirable beat. He landed it with the "short-stop run" that served up a host of stories: petty crimes from the 15th-street-police station, the suspect denizens and celebrities alike who passed through Union Station, and the results of accidents and other violence that made their way to the city hospital. Writing back to his family in November, he explained the scope of his new circuit: "This last week I have been handling a murder story, a lot of Police dope and the YWCA fund stuff a couple of times so am mixing em up."[14] Reporters who worked alongside Hemingway—such as Francis Davis, the later coauthor of the *Mr. and Mrs. North* detective novels, and John Selby, the eventual novelist and then editor-in-chief of Rinehart & Company—described him as always chasing after ambulances for a story.

What Hemingway witnessed during these Kansas City months offered material for his early efforts at fiction writing, much of which has been lost to literary history. In December of 1922, Hadley Richardson Hemingway, Papa's first of four wives, boarded a train at the Gare de Lyon in France. She was to join her husband on a skiing trip. After leaving a suitcase unattended

in her train compartment, Hadley returned to find it missing—
and along with it several manuscripts that Hemingway had been
working on while in Europe. Papa would never recreate the lost
stories, several of which concerned Kansas City.

He would later publish, however, two stories that did draw
upon the city he covered as a *Star* reporter. "A Pursuit Race"
describes an advance man for a burlesque show who, like Ole
in "The Killers," gives his life up to complacent fate in a Kansas City room, collapsed in alcoholism and sardonic love with a
bed sheet. "God Rest You Merry, Gentleman" is set in the recep-
tion room of the General Hospital. In the story, two ambulance
doctors (one inept, one taunting) recall a tormented boy who
attempted to castrate himself over his sexual guilt. The doctors'
inability to help the boy work through his emotional turmoil
recalls the hospital work covered in newspaper pieces such as
"At the End of the Ambulance Run," a description of the city-
hospital surgeons. Picking up the detritus of robberies, razor
fights, and charity cases, the doctors dealt with their patients
as indiscriminately as a mechanic fixing an automobile. "And so
the work goes on," wrote Hemingway.[15]

From these Kansas City experiences and the lessons he took
from Pete Wellington, Hemingway emerged from his *Star* training with a reporter's gift for capturing in writing what he witnessed in life. He could also use a reporter's ear for listening to
others and transforming their experience in the stories he told.
When later asked what defined good writing, Hemingway often
derided fellow authors who wrote about what they had read,
rather than what they had experienced. Such abstract writing,
he thought, was ornamental and stolid. Firsthand experience,
firsthand understanding should provide the uncut marble for
the writer's chisel.

It would be a mistake, however, to believe that Hemingway always lived first and wrote later. His vision of life was sharply defined by romantic ideas of manhood that shaped what he read, what he did, and what he wrote. He often exaggerated his adventures for the sake of a good story, whether they be a quick engagement to a movie star, his service during the Great War, or the cavorting he did with Left Bank friends. In his fiction—both literary and in letters home—Hemingway did not have a reporter's responsibility to truth. He had an artist's. For Papa, living and writing were inseparable. Life made fiction worth reading; fiction made life worth living.

Indeed, one might wonder, what could an American teenager, born outside of Chicago and learning journalism as his trade in Missouri, know about Italy to write a novel such as *A Farewell to Arms*? Enough to write about the horrors of World War I's Isonzo Front? To write convincingly about the Caporetto retreat that he did not actually witness? The Milan love affair between a wounded ambulance driver and his nurse?

The War Experience: Lessons in Life and Love

At the outbreak of World War I, Hugh Walpole joined the Russian Red Cross to work as a medic's assistant, after being rejected by the British Army due to his eyesight. His experiences during the "Great Retreat" from Galicia provided the basis for *The Dark Forest*, a novel about a Brit working along the Russian front for the Red Cross who is thwarted in his love for a nurse. The *New York Times* praised Walpole's novel as providing insight for Americans "far removed from the great war" who wanted to know its emotional impact upon those in it. The *Times* exclaimed that *The Dark Forest* was a "work of art so deeply rooted in reality."[16] *The New York Evening Sun* wrote of the romance, "Such a novel needed the war for its background. It needed the war for its origin."[17] The novel appealed in life-changing ways to the adolescent Hemingway.

Hemingway had always intended to join the same war that drew Walpole. After his arrival in Kansas City, he declared to his family that he would work until spring and then enlist. He wrote to his sister that the Army had turned him away on account of the poor vision that was his family's inheritance. The experiences of Walpole and Ted Brumback, a fellow *Star* reporter who had driven an ambulance in France during the war, suggested another route for Hemingway to make his way to the European fronts. Commissioned as a second lieutenant in the American Red Cross, Hemingway volunteered to serve along the Piave River front in northeast Italy. His job was to move amongst the entrenched line, distributing chocolate and cigarettes to the soldiers. In July of 1918, Hemingway was hit by shrapnel from an exploding trench mortar and then shot by Austrian machine-gun fire as he carried a wounded Italian soldier to safety. Just a year before he had been bumming around Michigan, not even having begun his reporter job for the *Star*.

Taken to a hospital in Milan, Hemingway came under the care of an older American nurse, Agnes von Kurowsky. Inevitably, he fell in love. She finally rejected him for an Italian officer. Such unrealized romance, while a source of torment, provided Papa with the emotional experience he would need to write *A Farewell to Arms* and such love-lost stories as "The Snows of Kilimanjaro."

In understanding what made Hemingway the author he was, it's important to understand how such passages of his life—and his life could be read as an adventure novel—shaped his sensibilities as a writer. *A Farewell to Arms* is no more a story about World War I than *Moby Dick* is about 19th-century whaling techniques. Nor is "The Snows of Kilimanjaro" about the snow mantle of Africa's highest mountain. These stories were about people's experiences, their emotions. Amidst a European war, an American ambulance driver struggles to court the woman he adores to find his love ultimately unrequited. Lying in an African camp, a dying writer lashes out at his wife, regrets the stories he won't live to write, and dreams of the peace of flight and Kilimanjaro's summit.

Habits of Hemingway While healing from his wounds in the Milan hospital, Hemingway composed stories on Red Cross stationery.

Before the wounds Hemingway took in battle and in love led to these later works, they made him something of a wartime celebrity in the press. He was hailed as the first American to be injured along the Italian lines, although this wasn't true. Upon his return home he took to delivering speeches at his old high-school auditorium and regaling the women of local social clubs. The extent of his wounds and the time he spent along the Italian front were often exaggerated by Papa in the accounts he gave at home and then later to his Parisian friends. For this reason the details of his injuries continue to be a source of debate for Hemingway's biographers attempting to distinguish the reality from the literature.

Hemingway himself, however, emphasized the power of a story to shape one's memory over a narrow fidelity to detail. In a letter to Charles Poore, who was preparing an introduction to a collection of Papa's work, Hemingway recalled that while recovering in the hospital from his wounds he most often listened to other soldiers and the stories they told. He explained, "Their experiences get to be more vivid than your own. You invent from your own and from all of theirs."[18] The key word for Hemingway, as an artist, was "invent." A reporter's responsibility, as he had learned in Kansas City, was to the facts and the type of truth found in science. An author, however, owed his responsibility to the creation of literature—the invention of good storytelling and the type of truth found in art. Papa had little patience when "some son of a bitch"[19] tried to discredit the importance of his stories by proving that he hadn't fought in a particular battle.

Early Efforts at Fiction and Sherwood Anderson

When he returned from World War I, Hemingway dedicated himself to becoming a fiction writer. He might have continued his work in journalism—and indeed, when first interviewed by the New York papers about his war experience, he offered them his services as a reporter. But he returned for a time to Oak Park, went fishing in Michigan, and then rented a second-floor apartment in Petoskey, Michigan, to focus on his writing. There, he settled into the daily work habits that he would follow for most of his life.

Rise early in the morning. Get to the typewriter. Write until about noon.

During the early Petoskey days, Hemingway worked odd jobs after lunch to earn his rent, or he chased after local girls. In later years, afternoons might be spent drinking at a café, fishing or swimming at a nearby spot, or playing with his boys. In

Cuba he wrote standing up, most often from his bedroom while Caribbean breezes came through the southern windows. But mornings were usually for writing. There were, of course, exceptions to this routine. In the burst of creativity that produced *The Sun Also Rises*, Hemingway wrote through lunch until the Madrid bullfights started. He hesitated to leave Spain and go to Paris while so hotly turning out prose. In a letter to Bill Smith, a childhood friend, Hemingway claimed that he was writing "like wildfire. . . . This book is going to crack right through."[21] Hemingway's commitment to his work—to honing his craft—was exacting. He tried multiple openings for *The Sun Also Rises* before settling into that novel's voice. And his dedication was shown in the seventy rewrites he attempted for the closing of *A Farewell to Arms*.

Habits of Hemingway Hemingway once explained to John Dos Passos that he was writing early each morning from 7 A.M. onward so that he could be outside during the summer afternoons. For the evenings? He wanted Dos Passos to join him and Hadley in Paris to go out drinking.[20]

The early work Hemingway produced upon his return from World War I imitated the tales of adventure he was reading in *The Saturday Evening Post*. As a whole, they showcase a manly-but-hollow action and the quick humor of cartoonish irony. Stories such as "The Passing of Pickles McCarthy" featured a prize-winning boxer who leaves the ring in order to fight with a hard-core Arditi regiment, wielding only a set of knives during the battle of Asolo. Ring Lardner, the Illinois newspaperman after whom Hemingway modeled some of his high school juvenilia, had found success with his satirical baseball stories in the *Post*.

It was natural, then, that the young Hemingway turned to this very popular and most American of magazines in an attempt to launch his fiction-writing career. It was also natural that the *Post* would overlook them, given their heavily wrought messages in place of subtle themes, and over-the-top caricatures in place of believable characters. The magazine rejected them all.

Hemingway continued to find success, however, in writing for newspapers, first in Toronto for the *Star Weekly* and then in Chicago as an editor for the *Co-operative Commonwealth*, the magazine of the Cooperative Society of America. However, two people whom Hemingway met while working in Chicago would change the course of his career: Sherwood Anderson, a well-known writer who had just returned from Europe; and Hadley Richardson, a St. Louis woman Hemingway met and married within ten months. Anderson was impressed by the young Hemingway's writing ability—describing him as "quite a wonderful newspaperman"[22]—and he convinced him that Paris was the place for an aspiring writer. Hadley was supportive of Hemingway's desire to return to Europe, and her recent inheritance from an uncle gave them enough money to do so.

The influence Anderson had upon Hemingway's writing can be seen most directly in Papa's "My Old Man," a coming-of-disillusionment story where a boy realizes the corruption of the horseracing world and his father's collusion with it. Hemingway's critics typically regard the story as derived from Anderson's "I Want to Know Why." Both stories do share important narrative qualities: they're told from the perspective of a naive adolescent in awe of racing horses. Their dramatic conflicts evolve from the natural purity of the sport and the mendacious culture that surrounds it. And their climaxes strip the narrators of both their enjoyment of the horseracing—to get "the kick out of it"—and their worship of an older father-figure.[23]

Stylistically, the two works are most similar in the use of the male teenage voice. Anderson postures the awkward announcements of a boy promising to tell his readers the point of a story without yet coming to the point, explaining what his mother "wouldn't of" let him do.[24] Hemingway uses the narrator's exclamation "Gee—" for his pronouncements of juvenile wisdom about the world. "My Old Man" had adopted some of the lessons of Anderson's writing to good effect, but Hemingway also made certain to make the story and style his own. As would be characteristic of Anderson's writing, his narrator blames his flawed role model's internal grotesqueness as the cause of his disenchantment. As would be characteristic for Hemingway, his narrator blames the world at large (and especially the influence of money) for his father's faults.

Whatever lessons Hemingway took from Anderson's work, he disavowed them in the years to come. While *Winesburg, Ohio* is Anderson's best-known work today, the only commercial success he saw during his lifetime was with *Dark Laughter* (1925). A novel about a Chicago news writer who leaves his wife to begin again in a New Orleans factory, it sold through eight printings in nine months and gave Anderson enough money to build the Virginian house he had long desired. Hemingway met the uneven *Dark Laughter* with disdain, however, and mocked Anderson's style in his parody *The Torrents of Spring* (1926). That Anderson had championed Hemingway's early talent only made the betrayal worse.

Boni and Liveright, Anderson's publishing company, rejected Hemingway's manuscript for *Torrents of Spring*, and forced Papa to find a new home at Charles Scribner's Sons, the company with which he would work throughout the rest of his life. The assault upon Anderson began a pattern of behavior that Hemingway would follow with other writers whom he initially looked to for guidance or embraced as peers, but later scorned as inferiors— Stein, Fitzgerald, and Dos Passos among them.

Gertrude Stein and Ezra Pound: Repetition and the Object Itself

As for steering him to a place to work on the craft of writing, Anderson had done well by Hemingway in guiding him to France. During the first half of the twentieth century, Paris's Rive Gauche, the Left Bank of the Seine River, burst with writers and painters, sculptors and musicians, experimenting with new stylistic techniques. For its literary community, Sylvia Beach's Shakespeare and Company, a bookstore and lending library, became a haven for writers such as Andre Gide, Paul Valery, Gertrude Stein, Scott Fitzgerald, John Dos Passos, Ezra Pound, T. S. Eliot, and James Joyce. After serialized portions of Joyce's *Ulysses* were censored in the United States and Britain over obscenity charges, Beach arranged the publication of the novel's first complete edition.

In an atmosphere of such literary innovation and freedom, the impecunious Hemingway first entered 12 rue de l'Odeon— Shakespeare and Company's location until Nazi occupation—in early 1921. Unable to buy his own books or join the lending library, he charmed Beach with stories of his wartime adventures and convalescence. She allowed him to put off paying the membership fee until he was able and let him borrow as many books as he liked. Among the first authors Hemingway read from her collection were Ivan Turgenev and D. H. Lawrence,

Leo Tolstoy, and Fyodor Dostoyevsky. In *A Moveable Feast*, Hemingway remembered Beach as the person who had always been kindest to him.

A Parisian Education

The first and, perhaps, most significant tutor for Hemingway's writing during these Paris years was Gertrude Stein. Anderson had introduced Hemingway to her as "an American writer instinctively in touch with everything worth-while going on here."[25] Where Anderson offered a model of writing founded upon the platitudes of theme, Stein taught Hemingway to think of writing as needing concentrated work and exacting technique.

In Paris, the apartment Stein shared with her partner, Alice B. Toklas, doubled as a private museum. There, with examples of Matisse's fauvism, Picasso's cubism, and Cézanne's postimpressionism, Hemingway could see paintings by members of the modernist avant-garde. These painters transformed the visual arts by experimenting with basic elements, the abstraction of color or the emphasis of geometric form. As such they are an important influence on the pared-down writing style Hemingway would develop in his masterpieces. He would later credit Cézanne's paintings with teaching him how to write landscapes.

The personal relationship Ernest and Hadley developed with Stein was warm and engaging at first. When the Hemingways had their first son, nicknamed "Bumby," Stein became his godmother. When their relationship turned to writing as a profession, Hemingway was eager for instruction in literary technique. Stein was eager for a student.

In an early study of Hemingway's formative years, Charles A. Fenton observed that what most prepared Papa for Stein's teaching was his lifelong interest in the technical aspects of any accomplishment, including boxing and bullfighting, football and fishing, warfare and writing.

A graceful technique could transform mundane method into art. Where Wellington had forced Hemingway to concentrate on his newspaper style, Stein focused him on his literary style.

But Stein and the circle of writers gathered around her also represented an acceptance into the literati that the boy from Oak Park lacked in his education. In foregoing college study, Hemingway learned his writing as a blue-collar trade in the newspapers for which he wrote. His style of prose was dictated by the pragmatism of covering news for a popular audience. Hemingway arrived in Paris, then, only with a portfolio of news items and human-interest stories, a sheaf of rejected manuscripts, and the endorsement of Sherwood Anderson.

By contrast, other American expatriates of the "Lost Generation" were exceptionally educated. Stein had graduated from Radcliffe, studied under William James, and had two years at Johns Hopkins Medical School before committing herself to the Montparnasse artistic community. Ezra Pound held degrees from Hamilton and the University of Pennsylvania, and had served for a time as W.B. Yeats's secretary. T.S. Eliot had earned both his bachelors and masters degrees from Harvard (studying under Santayana, Bergson, and Russell, among others). He failed to receive his PhD only when he refused to defend his dissertation after it had been accepted. Even Scott Fitzgerald, who was three years older than Papa, had spent those extra years at Princeton before enlisting in the Army.

The reading that Hemingway did at Sylvia Beach's bookstore and the teaching he accepted in Gertrude Stein's parlor, then, provided him with something of a more formal education to add to his experiences as a reporter and Red Cross volunteer.

Habits of Hemingway Papa relied upon the Shakespeare & Co. Bookstore and Sylvia Beach's kindness for the authors he read in Paris, such as Gogol and Chekhov. Other books that he read during his cold-water flat days included:

Fyodor Dostoyevsky, *The Gambler* (1887)

James Joyce, *Ulysses* (1922)

Leo Tolstoy, *War and Peace* (1869)

Ivan Turgenev, *A Sportsman's Sketches* (1852)

Stein was apt to think of herself as the voice of all twentieth-century literature, even as publishers and critics protested otherwise. She had a fondness for the dedicated Hemingway, though, and set about instructing him after an open invitation to visit her apartment anytime after 5 P.M. Hemingway responded well to her encouragement, much as he approved of Wellington's earlier discipline. In a letter, he explained that writing "used to be easy" before he had met her: "I'm awfully bad now but it's a different kind of bad."[26]

Stylistically, Stein's lessons stressed the role of rhythm and repetition in language. Her most famous line of poetry demonstrates both: "A rose is a rose is a rose is a rose."

Hemingway's early writing had shown the use of repetition, as in the repeated image of the hooker on a Kansas City street in "Mix War, Art and Dancing." There, the hooker's description serves as a framing device and counterpoint, only suggesting something of her loneliness. Under Stein's influence and after the maturing experiences of the war, Hemingway increasingly used repetition to suggest his characters' emotional experiences. Rather than the baroque alliteration he had used in that earlier newspaper piece, however, his repeated phrases became more brisk. Often, only one word or two. In "On the Quai at Smyrna," for instance, which opened the collection *In Our Time*, a narrator recalls the wartime horror of seeing women clinging to their "dead babies." In the two opening sentences of his fifth paragraph, Hemingway concludes each with the words "dead babies." In the third, he reinforces the image by reversing the words: "They'd have *babies dead* for six days."[27] As the narrator is haunted by this image—later contrasted with women giving birth to live babies—so are these sentences haunted by the words' repetition.

As Hemingway absorbed the lessons Stein taught him and adapted them into his own writing, the relationship between teacher and pupil upended. Many literary critics who championed Hemingway found that he had mastered the techniques of simple rhythms and effective repetition in ways that Stein herself never could. Her poetry emphasized the abstract resonances of language, particularly when it was good, but at its worst could be brazenly abstruse and unintelligible. Hemingway later claimed that Stein had learned to write effective dialogue from him, particularly under the influence of *The Sun Also Rises*. Stein would write that Hemingway learned to ape her theories but never had the wisdom to understand them.

Before their very public literary fallout, however, came a personal one. While the accounts of what led to the argument between the Hemingways and Stein differed over the years, it was likely Stein who broke off their friendship, most probably due to her lover's jealousy at the attention she gave Ernest. One day Hadley arrived with Bumby at Stein's apartment only to be told by Toklas that she was not available. The cut off was brief and final.

In her book, *The Autobiography of Alice B. Toklas* (1933), Stein assaulted both Hemingway's manhood and his writing, claiming both were a fraud. In her copy of *Death in the Afternoon* (1932), Hemingway inscribed: "A Bitch is a Bitch is a Bitch is a Bitch."[28]

Pound and the Imagists

Another major influence upon Hemingway's writing style during his Parisian education was Ezra Pound, the "better maker" to whom Eliot had dedicated *The Waste Land*. Pound was a strong advocate of literary talent when he saw it and was instrumental in getting much of Papa's early stories and poetry into print. In *A Moveable Feast*, Hemingway remembered Pound as a man who dedicated himself to others' art as much as his own.

Pound's role as mentor to Hemingway differed from Stein's in the way that the painter of miniatures differs from the landscape artist. Stein had worked with Hemingway on the broad strokes of language rhythms and the impressions they could leave upon a reader. She was notoriously unwilling to revise her work, however, perhaps due to ideas about inspiration and automatic writing that she took from William James. Hemingway attributed her disinterest to laziness. Pound, by contrast, focused Hemingway on the detail work of individual word choice, of getting the strongest impression possible from the fewest words. He taught Hemingway to carve out the unnecessary, particularly when it was designed only to showcase stylistic artifice. Hemingway respected him as "the man I liked and trusted the most as a critic then."[29]

Hemingway had asked Pound to review "An Alpine Idyll," which opens with the narrator and Jim returning from skiing before coming to the story of what a peasant has done with his wife's corpse over the winter. Pound critiqued the first pages for being too close to the poetic flourishes of Tennyson. Pound's advice? Come directly to the subject of the piece. He wrote to Hemingway in his manically playful way: "keep your eye on the objek MORE . . . ANYTHING put on top of the subject is BAD. Licherchure is mostly blanketing up a subject . . . The subject is always interesting enough without the blankets."[30]

Pound and Hemingway were very different writers. Pound's poetry traced itself back to Renaissance masters and Greek classics, the artistic past of European tradition. Hemingway's stories came from the boulevards of Paris and the bullfights of Madrid, the artist's experience in modern Europe. The two shared, however, very similar views about how language should work.

Papa Says While Hemingway found himself amid some of the world's most important writers in the 1920s, and would become a modern-day oracle for aspiring writers throughout his life, he thought of writing as a solitary project. "The further you go in writing the more alone you are."[31]

The Imagist movement of which Pound became a central part, along with Richard Aldington, Amy Lowell, and H.D. (Hilda Doolittle), emphasized the sharp image and compressed expression. The principles the Imagists established worked well with those Hemingway had absorbed from the *Kansas City Star* copy sheet: treat the subject directly, use "absolutely no word" that does not add meaning, and write in the rhythm of music, not the pretense of the metronome. Pound's definition that the poetic image should express "an intellectual and emotional complex in an instant of time," given a different context in prose, fits well with the techniques Hemingway would use in his own stories:[32] a riff on the repeated image of beer bottles in "An Alpine Idyll"; the complex of exchanged dialogue in "Hills Like White Elephants" or *The Sun Also Rises*.

But where Pound taught Hemingway how to whittle down a sentence, Hemingway taught Pound to throw a punch. Wyndham Lewis, whom Papa sparred with critically, described first meeting Hemingway in July of 1922: when he entered Pound's apartment, Lewis saw Papa fending off a fury of blows from his boxing pupil. Hemingway wrote to Howell Jenkins: "We have a hell of a good time. I'm boxing regular with Ezra Pound, and he has developed a terrific wallop."[33]

Habits of Hemingway Papa kept up a lifetime fondness for boxing. At times he exaggerated his own experience in the ring, claiming to have boxed with Sam Langford, the "Greatest Fighter Nobody Knows," and Harry Greb, "The Pittsburgh Windmill." At Bimini Beach, where Hemingway lived in the summer of 1935, he challenged any of the island's inhabitants to go three rounds with him. If they lasted, Papa would pay them a hundred dollars. Four tried, four failed. Others whom Hemingway sparred with:

Ezra Pound, poet and imagiste

Harold Loeb, model for Robert Cohen

Tom Heeney, professional heavyweight

Lewis Galantière, editor and translator

Wallace Stevens, poet

Morley Callaghan, novelist

Pound's personality was eccentric and often manic. Joyce once had to ask Hemingway to join them for a meal, afraid of their friend's odd behavior. But when Pound's Fascist radio broadcasts in World War II landed him a treason charge,

Hemingway joined the troop of artists who petitioned to save him by declaring him mentally unfit for trial. Many were writers that Pound had helped earlier in their careers, Eliot, Robert Frost, and Archibald MacLeish among them.

The break that Hemingway had with so many other writers, so many other friends, never came with Pound. Fitzgerald he later ridiculed as a child playing a man's game as a writer. Dos Passos he dismissed as a talent corrupted by wealth, especially in the caricature Papa saw of himself in *Chosen Country* (1951). Faulkner he thought good but criticized him for producing works that once read, couldn't be read again. Only Pound and Joyce survived Hemingway's opinion after the success of his own novels and his acceptance as a major literary figure.

Success, *The Sun Also Rises*, and A Farewell to Studenthood

From the early models of Lardner or Walpole to the mentoring of Wellington, Stein, and Pound, Hemingway's genius for storytelling came from his ability to recognize the best techniques from his teachers' lessons and to apply them to his own writing. By the mid-1920s, he found his success with the critically acclaimed *The Sun Also Rises* and the bestselling *A Farewell to Arms*. He began *The Sun Also Rises* on his birthday in 1925 and completed its first draft in Paris within two months. While traveling, he revised his work extensively and deliberately over the next six. By the time Scribner published the manuscript, Papa was separated from Hadley and would soon be divorced. The novel, considered his best by most critics, ensured Hemingway's reputation as a transforming talent in modern writing.

By 1928, Hemingway's apprentice years were over. He had relocated to Key West and was married to Pauline Pfeiffer, another expatriate with whom Papa carried on an affair while married to Hadley. In Florida, he kept up his habits of rising at first light and writing through the morning to produce *A Farewell to Arms*. While Papa drafted the novel, Pauline bore his second son, Patrick. Her troubled labor served as the model for Catherine Barkley's death during childbirth. While he revised the manuscript, his father committed suicide with a shot from a .32 Smith and Wesson. Hemingway's grandfather had carried the pistol during the American Civil War.

The publication of *A Farewell to Arms* brought Hemingway's reputation among literary critics to the peak of his eminence. The novel drew public accolades from the likes of Malcolm Cowley, T.S. Eliot, and Dorothy Parker. As America sank into the Great Depression in October of 1929, sales of *A Farewell to Arms* rose to more than 50,000 copies in two months, then 80,000 soon after. Hemingway's financial success from the book bought him a freedom to work and travel the world that few other writers shared. The dozen years that he lived in Key West were among his most prolific and saw the publication of works such as *Death in the Afternoon*, *Green Hills of Africa*, *Winner Take Nothing*, "The Short Happy Life of Francis Macomber," "The Snows of Kilimanjaro," and *The Fifth Column*.

The style of writing that Hemingway developed while in his mid-twenties became canonical, inspiring generations of future writers. It also ensured that Papa's later work, such as *Across the River and into the Trees* (1950), would be judged marginal in comparison to the writer at the height of his ability. Now we'll turn to the imitable elements of Hemingway's style to see what we can learn from him.

Mimicking Hemingway: A Host of Influences

While we're focusing on what Ernest Hemingway has to teach us about the art of writing, remember that all writers are influenced by a host of other books. This was certainly true of Hemingway, who read widely as a youth and always had a stack of books to read when he was a professional writer.

In this exercise, make a list of the stories by Hemingway you most admire. Then, make a list of other authors, either contemporary authors or otherwise, that you respect and would want to write like. Comparing the two lists, think about what similarities arise between the authors. Are you drawn to a particular type of character, perhaps the strong hero? Are you drawn to the subject matter, perhaps war or romance? Bullfighting or fishing? Is it the "voice" of the writers, the qualities of their writing that allow you to almost hear their words speaking from the page? Try mapping out what you most admire from the writers you know and keep those qualities in mind as we work through Hemingway's style.

A List to Avoid

Papa was also quick to point out what he detested in other writers' styles. Anything he didn't like—from a turn of phrase to a use of subject matter—could quickly become the source of ridicule in his own fiction. (Think of the sometimes novelist Robert Cohen in *The Sun Also Rises*.) Make a list of authors that you dislike, either for subject or style. Then, contrast those writers with Hemingway. What is it that those writers you'd rather dismiss are doing differently from Papa? Are there elements of style that these dismissed authors do share with Hemingway? Can you identify the qualities of writing that you would most like to avoid?

Taking Stock of Hemingway

Before we launch into the next chapters and see what made Hemingway's style unique, take the time to reread two or three Hemingway short stories that you've found most remarkable. (If you're new to Hemingway and unsure of which to start with, try these three: "The Killers," "Hills Like White Elephants," and "The Snows of Kilimanjaro.") Then, make a list of what stands out for you: What is it about Hemingway's sentence style that is so remarkable? Why do his characters seem so distinctive? What's distinctive about his characters' dialogue? What can you visualize about his settings and descriptions of character? What do you notice about the point of view of his narrators? Refer to this list as we work through these aspects of Papa's writing over the next chapters.

A Lean, Well-Honed Style: Writing Through *Papa's Voice*

2

"Mr. Hemingway knows how not only to make words be specific but how to arrange a collection of words which shall betray a great deal more than is to be found in the individual parts."

(Review of *The Sun Also Rises*)

After *The Sun Also Rises* was published in 1926, the style of any other novel simply got in the way of itself. Or so Hemingway had made it seem.

Readers of Henry James, for instance, found themselves amidst dense thickets of prose, with knotted passages of psychology enveloping each character. For anyone who passed through the pages of an Edith Wharton novel, snarling paragraphs on the rituals of metropolitan society awaited. And tangled vines of sentences wrapped around readers caught in chapters written by William Faulkner, Papa's rival and contemporary.

Hemingway's writing, by contrast, raced along a quickened path.

Consisting of chapters filled more with dialogue than heavy description, *The Sun Also Rises* speeded readers along highways of character exchanges. It taught writers that they could conjure description through an assembly of short, minimalist sentences. When the novel was first reviewed in the *New York Times*, what stood out was not only this sparse style but also an arrangement that made the writing seem something more than a gathering of bare words. The "great deal more" that the reviewer sensed beneath the surface was an early suggestion of what Hemingway came to call his "Iceberg Theory" of writing.

Since then, Hemingway's influence on the shape of American writing has been profound. His masculine heroes, chasing gallantry in an age that's lost it, or his female characters, flirting with the promise of sexual freedom, are immediately recognizable. His dialogue, freed from weighty description, sounds like no other writer's. His settings, written like landscapes, appear like a Cézanne canvas.

More than any of these other qualities of his writing, it's the terse richness of Hemingway's voice that makes him stand out among crowds of other writers. His style was built upon the hard sentence, sharpened to show the exactness of each word. Where other writers contrived complicated webs of syntax, Hemingway cut to the point. In learning how to write from other writers, you might best start with their techniques of narrator or character, building up to style as an afterthought to storytelling substance. But in learning from Hemingway, you must start with the style of his writing as a way to unlock his presentation of character, description, and storytelling.

We begin this chapter by examining the trademark tones that distinguished Hemingway's voice, beginning with the principles of brevity that Papa himself used to explain his writing technique. We'll see what Hemingway meant by his "Iceberg Theory" as a way of writing. We'll see how he began each day's work searching for "one true sentence" that allowed him to capture the "real thing" of life. And we'll look at the specific lessons Hemingway's work offers for sharpening our own well-honed style.

Writing as an Iceberg

When Hemingway talked about what guided his writing style, he referred to what he called his "Iceberg Theory." The idea was simple enough: as the visible part of an iceberg suggests an unseen depth below the surface, so writing should show as little as possible to suggest a world more complex than what appears on the page.

In a word, the Iceberg Theory commands writers to do one thing: omit.

Leave out anything nonessential to the emotion you're trying to create with a story. Leave out the overwhelming details that can drown a reader in tedium. Leave out backstory that can be guessed at in the action of a plot. Leave out cumbersome dialogue tags when conveying the voices of characters.

By cutting out stylistic fat, writers build up the muscle of a sentence. By keeping a sentence short, the strength of individual words becomes most potent. Limiting the exposed surface of a story allowed Hemingway to elegantly suggest the deep tensions of character and deeper experiences of life that he brought to his craft.

The Shape of the Iceberg: Defining Papa's Principle

Death in the Afternoon was Hemingway's nonfiction effort to capture the grace of the bullfighter in the ring, the art of the *torero*. The book also allowed Hemingway to give his first extensive public comments on the craft of writing. Doing so, he compared the rituals of the Spanish bullfight—where man-of-art dances with the animal-of-nature—with the traditions of literature— where a writer's talent dances with the language of experience.

It was in *Death in the Afternoon* that Papa explained what he meant by the Iceberg Theory. Since its principles so underscore all other elements of Hemingway's writing, it's worth emphasizing in detail:

> *If a writer of prose knows enough about what he is writing about he may omit things that he knows and the reader, if the writer is writing truly enough, will have a feeling of those things as strongly as though the writer had stated them. The dignity of movement of an ice-berg is due to only one-eighth of it being above water. A writer who omits things because he does not know them only makes hollow places in his writing. A writer who appreciates the*

seriousness of writing so little that he is anxious to make people see he is formally educated, cultured or well-bred is merely a popinjay.[34]

Here Papa lays out how writers should think of the style and subject of their writing, how they want readers to react to the words on the page, and the possible missteps that a writer can make in interfering with that reaction.

The Iceberg Theory can be summarized in four principles:

1. Write About What You Know, But Don't Write All That You Know
2. Grace Comes from Understatement
3. Create Feelings from the Fewest Details Needed
4. Forget the Flamboyant

As a matter of style, the Iceberg Theory explains the reason behind Hemingway's terse voice. Its idea of the barely visible demands the short sentence. But these principles also touch upon every other aspect of Hemingway's writing: from the depth of character, to the cadence of a dialogue; from the vision of a landscape, to the shape of a story. Understanding the iceberg principles, then, can offer something of a philosopher's stone by revealing the lessons Hemingway's work has to teach us as writers. Let's examine each of these principles for what they suggest about how you should prepare yourself to write and the language you should use in creating a story.

Papa Says In his advice to the starving writer, who hopes an audience will come to understand new genius, Hemingway offered: "Hunger is good discipline and you can learn from it."[35]

Write About What You Know, but Don't Write All That You Know

Creative writers are often told: Write about what you know. It is simply impossible for authors to write believably about what they don't know, haven't thought through, or haven't adequately imagined. A writer who has scant knowledge of the Sawtooth Mountains cannot convincingly write about Papa's Ketchum, Idaho. A writer who has never seen a bull lower its shoulders to thrust its mass toward a taunting *muleta* cannot get what Papa called the "real thing" into a story.

Hemingway's success as a writer came in large part from his self-knowledge of what he could convincingly write stories about. In 1928, he had completed more than 45,000 words of a novel, *Jimmy Breen*, that he told Maxwell Perkins would be a type of contemporary *Tom Jones*. But he expressed doubt to Perkins that he knew enough then to write such a book. He doubted whether he would ever know enough to write such a book. He claimed, rightly so, that his previous writing accomplishments had come from writing only what he knew about.[36] This was after the success of *The Sun Also Rises*. *Jimmy Breen* was set aside, never published by Hemingway in his lifetime. Hemingway instead wrote his next novel from a wartime knowledge of human injury and intimacy. That novel, *A Farewell to Arms*, secured his reputation as one of the greatest writers of English prose.

How do you gain enough knowledge to write a story? How do you know enough to write a complete novel?

A writer's knowledge can come from experience or it can come from reading. For Hemingway, it came from both. Hemingway became most famous for writing about the experiences he threw himself into: the social circles of Paris and Pamplona, the horrors and love of World War I, the adventures of the African safari. But he also researched the history and culture of Spanish bullfighting to prove himself an aficionado of its art. Despite having served and been wounded at the Italian front, he researched details of the Caporetto retreat to flesh out the setting of *A Farewell to Arms*.

Habits of Hemingway Hemingway once wished he had been able to write about airplanes, but William Faulkner had written well about pilots in novels such as *Soldier's Pay* and *Pylon*. Not one to repeat what another writer had already accomplished, Hemingway left the skies to his Mississippi rival.[37]

Fiction writers have the benefit of creating characters and stories entirely from the imagination. But Hemingway warned against either purely making up or leaving out what you don't know in writing. Doing so sounded a hollow thud in the body of a writer's work, an obvious omission that readers would sense as false. He chastised Fitzgerald for altering the parents and upbringing of characters that had been based on real people. If a person came from a lawyer father and schoolteacher mother, his fictional characterization must come from the same stock. Anything changed would produce the unbelievable.

In his own writing, Hemingway often stayed religiously close to the experiences from which he invented his stories. He explained to Charles Scribner that writers must invent to give their stories depth, but that all such imagining had to be grounded in the writer's knowledge of the world.

Here's the trick to Hemingway's technique: Once you know the subject of your story in depth, leave most of what you know out.

If you include everything that you know about your material—from character revelations to the turns of a plot to the facets of setting to historical nuances—your stories will seem shallow. This idea may seem counterintuitive: if you include more, shouldn't your writing seem deeper? Not quite.

The depth of a fictional world is an illusion. The more you can suggest a world beyond what's spelled out on the page, the greater that world will seem. (This is distinct from specifying a narrow world limited only to what's on the page.) What you suggest in a story builds anticipation amongst your readers. What you can hint at but leave out, builds mystery.

Beginning writers often rush to include everything they know about a subject. In trying to show how much they know, more often than not they show that it amounts to little.

An example of Hemingway leaving aside much of his knowledge to write a story is found in *The Old Man and the Sea*. Focusing on old man Santiago and his fight with the marlin, Hemingway left out other stories of his ocean experiences and stories from the Cuban fishing village that other writers might have included. Hemingway might have included the visions of marlin breeding habits or enormous schools of sperm whales that he claimed to have witnessed in the Atlantic. He might have included stories of the other fishermen who come to respect Santiago after he hauls the picked-apart carcass of his trophy to port. In being able to leave these detours from the story unwritten, Hemingway focused the story on the experience of Santiago's sea, not the diversions of fish or people around him.

Exercise: Pruning Your Knowledge

Select a subject with which you're intimately familiar. You might, for instance, begin with the hometown where you grew up. (As Hemingway was making his way as a writer in Paris during the early 1920s, he often returned to the Michigan of his family's summers for his subject matter.) Sketch out a list of everything you know on that subject, from the people involved, to its specific language. Your list doesn't need to be comprehensive, but try to get a sense of the depth of your knowledge. When you're done, scan down the page for what you think would make for a story worth writing—either a promising start for a work of your imagination or an event worth shaping in a nonfiction story. Then, cross out whatever details seem unrelated to what makes that story interesting. As you come up with the material for one story, repeat as necessary. You might use these story ideas as we move on to exercises about character and dialogue in future chapters.

What's the Point? Many people are so fascinated with the details of a subject they're interested in that they aren't able to filter out what's important to someone to whom they're telling a story. Writers must select only what's important. For Hemingway, that's minimally so.

Grace Comes from Understatement

Hemingway's writing frequently produced a kind of male character, the "code hero" (see Chapter 3). The hero was that type of character, found in Jake Barnes or Robert Jordan, who met life's tragedies quietly and with dignity. It's no coincidence, then, that Hemingway treated his rule of omission as a type of stoic order that defined the style of writing appropriate for American authors. For Papa, the principles of the Iceberg Theory formed the code of professional prose.

The personal letters that Hemingway wrote to friends and family, by contrast, show a remarkably different style of writing, one filled with his judgments, convictions, and condemnations. When Horace Liveright accepted the manuscript for *In Our Time*, Hemingway's early collection of short stories, the publisher asked that "Up in Michigan" be cut out due to its too direct treatment of sex. Hemingway wrote "The Battler" to take that story's place in the collection, and his letters to friends about the new work effused with his thoughts on the quality of the replacement. In letters to Liveright and John Dos Passos, he boasted about how the story pulled the collection together. Writing to F. Scott Fitzgerald about a mutual friend he didn't want to offend so as to add to the regrets that kept him up at night, Hemingway referenced his Battler's mutilated ear as the scarred symbol for a life of suffering. These types of judgments about how good or bad something might be, or what a symbol represented, were precisely what Hemingway struggled to keep out of his fiction.

"The Battler" follows Nick Adams as he meets an ex-prizefighter, Adolph Francis, and his jailhouse friend, a black man named Bugs. After Nick is tossed from the train and stumbles into the woods, he catches a fire-lit glimpse of Ad's mangled face. In the trademark piece-by-piece lean sentences the writer became known for, Hemingway describes each of Ad's distorted features. Nose. Eyes. Mouth. Coloring. Pulverized first ear. Missing second.

Hemingway emphasizes Ad's physical description. He mentions—briefly—Nick's reaction, first embarrassed at being caught staring and then sickened at the sight of Ad's head. What Hemingway doesn't do is wax philosophically over either the nobility or stupidity of Ad's boxing. When Ad's temper turns violent over a dispute about Nick's knife, Hemingway describes the physical action, the movements of boxer and boy. He doesn't play psychologist or explain what emotions set Ad off. When Bugs later tells Nick the rumors that Ad had married his sister, Hemingway keeps to the dialogue. He doesn't interrupt with a voice-of-God narrator descending to judge right from wrong. He doesn't, in short, insert the types of personal judgments that characterized his letters.

Hemingway's code heroes accepted life's tragedies as they came. They accepted the triumphs with the same stolid resolve. In the style of writing that privileged what Maxwell Perkins called Hemingway's "objective" method, the dignity of the Iceberg Theory held that you should present a scene for your readers with the same acceptance of reality that such characters had. Write, don't judge.

Save the moralizing for priests and professors. If you need to pronounce upon your subject, do it to your friends and not in the work.

Exercise: Suspended Sentence

Go back to the subject list you generated in the previous exercise. Now, make a list of all the opinions you have on the subject—which actions are unfair, which people are detestable, which are to be praised. After you've made this list, be certain to keep these types of pronouncements out of your story. Stick to character, dialogue, description, and action.

What's the Point? Hemingway hated sentimentality in stories. By identifying your own opinions before you write the story, you'll be better able to keep out such sentiment. This doesn't mean that you can't make a character out to be the villain, but you should do so by showing the character's actions, not in telling readers to think of him as the villain.

Create Feelings from the Fewest Details Needed

Another maxim frequently told to beginning writers is: Show, don't tell. When writers start out, they often tell their readers too much, show them too little. That is, they tell readers that a character was thrown from a train. They don't provide enough details-in-words for readers to visualize the experience, to feel the push from the car or the impact of the ground.

Papa Says In a letter to Arther Mizener, Hemingway wrote, "Writing is a rough trade *et il faut d'abord durer* (and first you need to last)."[38] Persevere through both the good and the bad writing, the good and the bad reviews. Hemingway used that phrase throughout his life, inscribing it in both letters and copies of books that he gave to friends.

As they learn that lesson, however, some writers rush to the opposite extreme. They include every detail conceivable in an orgy of description. Readers are often overwhelmed, distracted, and annoyed by the inability of the writer to select which details matter most and leave out the rest.

Hemingway's advice—and what set his style apart from other writers—was to pare down a scene to its minimally essential parts.

The opening of Hemingway's "The Battler" strikes such a balance in showing enough detail but holding back from overly pronouncing the action. In the story's first paragraph, Nick stands up to see a train's caboose pulling away. In the second paragraph Hemingway describes the wounds on Nick's knee and hands. It's not until the third paragraph that Papa recounts the event that landed Nick on a railroad bed, being thrown from the train by a brakeman. Wounded effect comes before a description of what caused it. As Nick pauses to take in his fresh injuries, so must readers slowly make sense of them without knowing what brought them about.

In describing Nick's injuries, Hemingway writes:

> *He felt of his knee. The pants were torn and the skin was barked. His hands were scraped and there were sand and cinders driven up under his nails.*[39]

Notice that Hemingway selects one word to describe each of Nick's injuries. The description is slim but sufficient: Pants-were-torn. Skin-was-barked. Hands-were-scraped. (And is there a better word to described Nick's skinned knees than "barked"?) The rhythm of the short-phrasing sets each clause aside as readers take in the damage to his body. When we arrive at the longer, last part of the sentence, that clause's comparative length ("sand

and cinders") suggests the amount of variegated dirt jammed under his fingernails.

Imagine if Hemingway had been too short, too general:

Nick's pants were ripped, his knees and hands bloodied. Dirt had been driven under his nails.

Here we move too quickly over the details. The description is vague and lifeless. It tells too much, shows not at all.

Imagine also if Hemingway had overindulged his description:

Nick touched his bruised and battered knee. The pants were ripped across their width, seam to seam, in two shredded ribbons of fabric, swaying from where they were attached at the side. The leg underneath was shaved of its bark, jagged patches exposed and already scabbing. His hands were filleted into combed rivulets of blood, and there were fine sand and coarse cinders driven up under his darkened nails.

Such a description uses twice the words but achieves half the effect. It pauses too often to dwell on unneeded detail. Where Hemingway preferred rich and meaningful nouns, this description tries to achieve life through hollow adjectives. Too much gasping at airy adjectives, however, leaves it overwritten and dying.

Developing a style modeled on Hemingway's Iceberg Theory, then, means finding a sense of what makes for a "true" description. Avoid a description so sparse as to be unimaginative, but neither should you build a laundry list of ridiculous adjectives.

Exercise: Embellishing Hemingway

Select two or three sentences of description from another of Hemingway's stories. You might focus on "Soldier's Home," with Krebs's description of the girls; "The Last Good Country," with Nick Adams and his sister Littless; or "God Rest You Merry, Gentlemen," with its Kansas City snow-filled streets. Now, experiment with embellishing Papa's minimalist description, as we've done with "The Battler." Add adjectives where Hemingway has none. Add metaphors where Hemingway provides stark detail. Add poetic flourishes of phrase where Papa offers the hard and direct. When you're done, contrast your embellished version of those sentences against Hemingway's original. Can you sense why Papa chose the words that he did and no others?

What's the Point? Picking out only the essential details of your writing requires establishing a sense of when you're overwriting. In contrasting your overwrought description with Papa's original, you should begin to sense why Hemingway's sentences don't need such ornaments.

Forget the Flamboyant

When Hadley Hemingway lost the suitcase that contained most of her husband's work in 1924, among the manuscripts and their carbon copies, Hemingway claimed, was a complete novel and several other stories. While the loss devastated him at the time, Papa later thought that the experience helped the development of his writing skill. The slate of his early writing was cleared. Hemingway was free to give up what he called the "lyric facility" of his youth.[40]

What Hemingway saw in his early writing was an affinity for the overly artful. The bulk of his work gone, Papa reinvented his style to become the writer we know today.

As a writer of natural talent and an avid reader, the young Hemingway easily picked up the tricks of "literariness": The musicality of a phrase, the thrill of an action, the unity of a "perfect" ending. That skill can be seen in stories he wrote at the *Kansas City Star*, as in "Mix War, Art and Dancing." For the title of a story he wrote in Toronto, "The Ash Heel's Tendon," Hemingway made a sophomoric reference to Achilles's Heel and exuberantly attracted attention to his bookishness. The story's improbable plot turns on an assassin being caught by the police because of his love of Italian opera, his exposed tendon of vulnerability.

As Hemingway explains in his dismissal of overeducated flamboyance, the purpose of serious writing isn't to demonstrate how much you know. Readers will not be dazzled by your ability to flaunt a far-flung reference to ancient myths in your stories. Save that for your school writing.

Consider, for instance, the mature style Hemingway showed in "The Undefeated," a story about the injured bullfighter Manolo who struggles to return to the ring. As the *torero* performs before a charging bull, a displeased crowd, and a second-string newspaper critic, Hemingway's sentences stick to the short declarations for which he became known. In many paragraphs, the sentences average between six and ten words. They follow a genuinely simple pattern. Gone from Hemingway's style were the sentences complicated for the sake of complication. When Hemingway did break into a long, complexly wrought sentence, it was for good purpose. As Manuel swings his cape and side-steps a bull, Hemingway uses one long, fluid sentence—building phrase upon phrase—stretched out to almost 100 words. The length and rhythm of the sentence suggests the exchange between bullfighter, bull, and picador in one elegant movement.

Habits of Hemingway Hemingway's satiric portrayal of an ignorant bullfight critic in "The Undefeated" was not accidental. More than one literary critic had been unkind about Hemingway's art, and he was still having difficulty placing his stories. Both *the Dial* and the *Saturday Evening Post* turned down "The Undefeated."

Beginning writers often rush to show every trick of language they've ever learned in their writing. It's only natural, after all, to use a new tool that they've been given. Doing so might prove them apt pupils for a writing workshop. But a bag of literary tricks will no more build a story than a sack of tools will build a house. As Hemingway saw it, building a story that resonated with people required the basic bricks and mortar of engaging characters and good storytelling.

Exercise: One Word

Select an object that you'd like to include in a story, something that's rich in history. A baseball glove that's been passed down by a Cuban family who played at Finca Vigía. A flea-market suitcase from France that hasn't been opened in more than eighty years. The Springfield rifle that your character's grandfather used in the Civil War. Now write a paragraph giving its physical description, and be as flamboyant as you like. Get the excessive out of your system. Detail each knick, each smoothened edge, each corner calling out for an adjective. When you're done, do away with this description, too rich for Hemingway's taste. Select one adjective, one true word, for the object that suggests the rich depth that you've just sketched, but does so without a fancy turn of phrase.

What's the Point? Hemingway was a minimalist. That means choosing the least to carry the greatest. Your one final word should be the tip of the iceberg—your overly rich paragraph must lie unseen beneath the surface.

Learning to Write with the Iceberg Theory

How did Hemingway develop this Iceberg Theory? When did he first begin to write after the principle of the iceberg?

The story of how Hemingway came to this style of writing winds its way through his days at the *Kansas City Star* and the influence of writers such as Gertrude Stein and Ezra Pound. But Hemingway claimed to have begun practicing it with "Out of Season," a short story written after Hadley lost his manuscripts at the Gare de Lyon.

"Out of Season" follows Peduzzi, a voluble, old fishing guide, as he leads a quarrelling married couple to a local fishing spot, even though it's illegal to fish for trout at that time of year. The couple bickers back-and-forth, continuing a mysterious argument they had over lunch. When they learn the distance to the fishing spot, the wife abruptly turns back. But after arriving at the river, the husband is relieved to have forgotten the necessary lead weights for his line, and he too heads back to their hotel. Despite Peduzzi's promises to take them fishing the next day, the husband explains that he probably won't be going. There the story ends.

In a Christmas Eve letter to Fitzgerald, however, Hemingway insisted that the real ending of "Out of Season" was the fishing guide's suicide.[41] He hangs himself after being fired for drunken incompetence, claimed Hemingway. Papa explained that he left out this dramatically different ending because he didn't think the story needed it. He was trying to write a tragic story with no violence. Papa repeated his claim decades later in *A Moveable Feast* when he explained that a writer could omit anything if he knew what was being left out. This should be done only if the part left out helped suggest an emotion to readers without them quite knowing from where that feeling came.

It's difficult to see how Peduzzi's hanging would fit into "Out of Season." There is no detail, no hint of his personality that would make such a suicide believable for this character.

Hemingway wrote that the exchange between husband and wife was taken near verbatim from a dispute that he had with Hadley. The story's narrative is invested most heavily in the husband and wife's simmering tensions, the unexplained reason why they are so displeased with each other. Peduzzi adds a bumbling, comic presence to their argument—talking to them in alternating, rapid-fire Italian and German dialects because he doesn't know which they understand. To end with his suicide would draw the story away from the couple, unbalance the narrative from couple to guide, and appear as an abrupt non sequitur tacked on to the end.

Some of Hemingway's critics discount the idea that the real-life model for the fishing guide who killed himself is another of Papa's exaggerations, like the wartime stories he invented about leading Arditi troopers up Monte Grappa. One biographer goes so far as to suggest that Papa invented the story of the quarreling couple entirely, supposing that Hemingway's adherence to a "code" of proper sport wouldn't allow him to fish from illegal streams.

But even if Hemingway fabricated the story of the guide's death as the "real ending," his doing so indicates how he thought of his story as the pared-down snapshot of a greater portrait. As his Iceberg Theory would hold, each scene of a story should suggest more tension than it states. Hemingway's comments on the cut-off ending of "Out of Season" also distracts us from the underlying tension that is suggested in the story but goes unresolved: the reason for the couple's argument. It may be that their bickering comes from the illegal and unpleasant fishing trip, but the husband's apologies for the way he talked over lunch and the wife's hearing the word "doctor" when Peduzzi says "daughter" suggest something more.

Applying the Iceberg Theory

If "Out of Season" was Hemingway's first use of the Iceberg Theory—coming after the need to reinvent himself due to the loss of his manuscripts—he would perfect the art of the left-out in stories to come. "Big Two-Hearted River" would suggest the horrors of World War I while never mentioning them. "Hills Like White Elephants" would pit a couple arguing over an "abortion" while never using the word.

Exercise: An Ending, Cut Out

Write a scene of two to three pages that leads up to a dramatic event, perhaps a romance that's finally requited, a fight between characters that leads to one's death, or a couple's argument that ends their relationship. Pick out details of character, dialogue, and action that suggest but do not directly state this ending. Then, leave the dramatic ending out. To test your skills of suggestion, give your story to two or three readers and ask them what they think should happen to the characters after the scene. The idea with this exercise is to see how well the details you provide build up to what you leave out. If your readers pick out what you had planned, that's a sign that you're leading them along the way. Be careful of being too directive. If readers have no doubt about what will happen, that may be a result of too controlling a suggestion.

What's the Point? Hemingway thought that what you leave out of a scene should power the emotion or suspense of what's left in. If readers don't pick out the plot turn you left out, it may be that your writing is suggesting something else—perhaps as the guide's death doesn't quite add up from what happens in "Out of Season."

The Beginning Sentence, Alone and True

In *A Moveable Feast*, a memoir of his Paris years, Hemingway recalled the anxieties he faced in his apartment each morning over beginning to write for the day. He had always found ways of starting before, and looking over the city's rooftops, he reassured himself that he would find a way to begin then. Other writers began with introductions or prefaces, useless fanfare that avoided the thing of substance, the charge of the bull. Hemingway began with the "one true sentence."

His time at the *Kansas City Star* had taught him to write a basic declarative sentence. That lone sentence, standing by itself, formed the essential element of Hemingway's style. He would call that training the best that a writer could get, if he could leave the newspaper business before it affected his art.

But what did Hemingway mean by a sentence being "true"? How does the newspaper's short declarative sentence become art? Serious writing, as Hemingway thought of it, attempted to get at the "real thing," a sense of emotion gained from the world. In *Death in the Afternoon*, Hemingway contrasted the writing found in newspapers with writing that presented the reality of emotional experience. Newspaper writing tells you what happened on a given day and its style makes it timely for that day only. Literature, however, gives you the world in all its "sequence of motion and fact" so that the emotion comes whether you read it that day or again ten years later. As Ezra Pound explained, "Literature is news that STAYS news."[42]

A Key to Hemingway's Style

The characteristic of what defined Hemingway's short and true style might be summarized as follows:

- Write objectively, describing details of the world not emotions.
- Break the details of an object (or a scene) into their basic elements.
- Emphasize nouns.
- Choose active verbs, not passive ones.
- Adjectives, few but apt.
- Keep sentences short.
- Stick with basic grammar.
- Write complex sentences to speed up action, describe flowing motion, or to allow those short, basic sentences to stand out.
- Depend upon dialogue to draw characters.
- Use common vocabulary.
- Use repetition to remind readers what they've read.
- Seldom use similes.

Check off these characteristics in your mind as we read through this next paragraph from "The Battler." Here, Nick Adams has stumbled out of the woods to see Ad Francis for the first time:

> *The man looked at Nick and smiled. In the firelight Nick saw that his face was misshapen. His nose was sunken, his eyes were slits, he had queer-shaped lips. Nick did not perceive all this at once, he only saw the man's face was queerly formed and mutilated. It was like putty in color. Dead looking in the firelight.*[43]

Notice that Hemingway begins with the objective details of the scene, moving later to what Nick couldn't perceive. Nouns dominate, typically taking one adjective. Two adverbs are used, "only" and "queerly." The sentences average less than ten words in length over the paragraph. The first five clauses average less than six words each. The clauses follow a basic subject-verb-object pattern. The sentence about Nick's vague impression—he's unable to see the details Hemingway describes—stretches out to nineteen words. Balanced around a comma splice, this longer sentence allows the shorter ones to stand out. The diction used could be overheard on any street. The words "firelight," "queer," and "face" each repeat once to remind us what goes on in the paragraph. One simile is used ("like putty"). It's short, direct, and appeals to another direct object (the putty).

In that one paragraph, concentrated, we have all but one of the characteristics that define the Hemingway style. Scan through "The Battlers" heavy use of dialogue to pick up this last characteristic. You might notice Nick's excited exclamation points against Ad's gruff declarations.

As we turn next to why Hemingway's style was so revolutionary, keep in mind how this return to basic elements—writing that makes the stone *stony*—competed against the complex Victorian sentences common in the century before him.

Exercise: Hearing Hemingway

Perhaps the quickest way to pick up a sense of Hemingway's style is to hear it. Select one of Papa's stories, perhaps "The Battler," "The Undefeated," or "Out of Season." Then, read it aloud, or ask someone else to read it aloud to you. Or, better yet, listen to an audio recording of Hemingway's complete stories. As you're listening, read along with the printed word. Notice how the key characteristics of Hemingway's style can change the rhythm, emphasis, and character of the story's voice.

What's the Point? While we often talk about "hearing" a writer's voice on the page, there's nothing like reading the work out loud to pick up how the length of sentences or particular word choices translate into style. After you've completed three or four of the writing exercises in this book, you should then get in the habit of listening to your own work read aloud, preferably by someone else.

A Well-Honed Style

Green Hills of Africa (1935) was Hemingway's experiment in applying his writing techniques to an account of a safari he took between 1933 and 1934. Against charges that his earlier novels were closer to autobiography than art, the book also allowed Hemingway to distinguish his nonfiction from his stories of imagination. In doing so, he pronounced upon both the quality of his contemporaries' work and upon American writers of the past.

To understand the impact Hemingway's prose had upon literature, it's helpful to contrast Papa's style against that which came before him.

Earlier American writers had been "skillful." Edgar Allan Poe, with his excessively complex sentences, fit into this category with a mastery of what Papa saw as rhetoric. Judging Poe's writing, Hemingway found it "skillful, marvelously constructed," but ultimately "dead."[44]

"Dead" may be a sharp description of Poe, the writer who brought us "The Murders in the Rue Morgue" and "The Masque of the Red Death." But Hemingway didn't mean this as a compliment. Papa criticized Poe because he drew his material from fancy—invented from rhetoric and literariness, rather than reality and truth.

To see the difference in style between these two American writers, check out the opening sentence of Poe's "The Fall of the House of Usher":

> *During the whole of a dull, dark, and soundless day in the autumn of the year, when the clouds hung oppressively low in the heavens, I had been passing alone, on horseback, through a singularly dreary tract of country; and at length found myself, as the shades of the evening drew on, within view of the melancholy House of Usher.*

In one ambitious sentence, Poe establishes day, season, atmosphere, speaker, transportation, and setting. At the beginning, we have an entire "soundless" fall day whose evening approaches near the sentence end. In compressing a full day to one sentence, however, Poe must leave out certain descriptive details. In place of a visual description of the clouds overhead, we are given a feeling, an abstraction, of oppressiveness. In place of a description of the countryside, we are given the speaker's sentiment, that it was "singularly dreary." This technique is intentional on Poe's part. His narrator goes on through the paragraph to explain how the combined details of a setting come together to create a "sorrowful impression," a sensation that might be otherwise if aspects of the "melancholy" House of Usher had been arranged differently.

Hemingway's critique of Poe's style was that the earlier writer depended too heavily upon gimmicks. Poe wrote out of the fanciness of language. Papa wrote out of the truth of experience.

Rhetorically, Poe's sentence is very tight. It frames itself with the whole of a day climaxing with the presence of the House of Usher. Skillfully constructed, its controlling device, however, was a succession of "d" sounds, the trick of alliteration that united "dull," "dark," "soun-d-less day" "dreary," and "drew." Poe's genius as a writer was that he could use such techniques to suggest the hypnotizing states of mind of his characters, the disturbed atmospheres of a setting. The rhythm of sentences in "House of Usher" or the cadence of lines in "The Raven" echoed with the haunted sounds of a traumatized dream-state. Poe's style of writing was grotesque, not in the sense of "disturbing" but rather in the fashion of an image distorted into absurdity or caricature.

The myth of Hemingway's writing is that he had used these overly artful techniques as a journeyman writer but had largely given them up by the time his writing matured during his Paris years. Alliteration and internal rhyme, such as Poe had used, were solely the product of his high school and Kansas City days. The truth of Hemingway's style, however, is more complex. As we'll see, he continued to use such literary devices, but did so more subtly.

A Different Approach

Contrast the opening of "The Fall of the House of Usher" with Hemingway's opening in *For Whom the Bell Tolls*. Much like Poe's beginning, Hemingway introduces a central character traveling along a mountain setting. Poe's narrator comes upon the ancestral home of his friend, Roderick Usher. Hemingway's central character, Robert Jordan, scans down the mountainside to rest his eyes upon a mill:

> *He lay flat on the brown, pine-needled floor of the forest, his chin on his folded arms, and high overhead the wind blew in the tops of the pine trees. The mountainside sloped gently where he lay; but below it was steep and he could see the dark of the oiled road winding through the pass. There was a stream alongside the road and far down the pass he saw a mill beside the stream and the falling water of the dam, white in the summer sunlight.*[45]

Notice that, like Poe, Hemingway's first sentence has a type of rhetorical unity, not the unity of time over a day but here a unity of space from the forest floor to its roof. Instead of condensing the particulars of day, atmosphere, and season into one moment, Hemingway breaks down the details of his scene into individual sentences. Character and forest first. Then mountainside and road. Then stream, mill, and waterfall. It is this minimalist attention to the individual parts of scene and description, character and dialogue, that distinguishes Hemingway's modern style.

What's missing from Hemingway's opening description of the Guadarrama countryside is a characterization of mood. Poe's narrator proclaims the emotions of his surroundings; they're oppressive, dreary, and melancholic.

Habits of Hemingway Papa kept track of his work by charting the number of words he wrote during a day, writing the total count on a piece of cardboard. While living in Cuba, he averaged perhaps 400 or 500 words per day, but would occasionally write more to justify taking a day off for fishing.

The eloquence of alliterative language is still present in Hemingway's technique, but his more understated use of alliteration sets him apart from Poe. He avoids striking the reader with that rapid-fire series of "d" sounds with which Poe opens. In Hemingway's first sentence, though, comes the "f" sounds: "flat," "floor," "forest," and "folded." The rest of the paragraph carries a succession of "p" sounds: "pine-needled," "to-p-s," "pine," and "pass." At the close of the novel, where Robert Jordan also lies down, the final sentence echoes these same soft "f" and "p" resonances. In contrast with Poe, then, Hemingway uses a similar technique but to different effect: Poe's quick repetition created a sense of mesmerism. Papa's extended technique blends the "f" and "p" sounds to evoke the settled place of a Spanish forest.

Stylistically, Poe's writing was dominated by the weighty use of such rhymed repetition. As we'll see in the coming chapters, Hemingway's minimalist style toned down such artful language. It emphasized instead the suggestion of personality through sparse details, the free flow of dialogue in quick exchange between characters, and a description grounded in the concrete.

The century that separated Poe and Hemingway's writing styles saw dramatic changes in both the history of the nation and the shape of its literature. When Poe first published "House of Usher" in 1836, the tract of country that would become Hemingway's home town sat undeveloped. The following year, however, the Galena and Chicago Union Railroad cut through the land and brought about what became Oak Park, Illinois. As the American landscape was so dramatically changed by the forces of the rail line, so Hemingway's writing helped to bring the country's literature into the modern era.

Exercise: Transforming Poe into Papa

Take the details of Poe's opening paragraph in "The Fall of the House of Usher" and rewrite them as if Hemingway had invented the scene. For inspiration, you might look to the short sentences found in the openings of "Hills Like White Elephants" or "The Three-Day Blow." Try keeping details such as the time of day, the time of year, the overhanging clouds, the lone journey on horseback, and the appearance of the house. In place of Poe's one long sentence, try breaking those details about day, season, clouds, and horse into their own separate sentences, separate pieces of a picture. Throw out abstractions such as "dreary," "oppressive," or "melancholy."

What's the Point? The goal here is to play with the differences in style between two very different writers. To see Hemingway's preference for understatement, rewrite the "House of Usher" sentence out of Poe's sing-song voice and into Papa's short-and-direct one. Developing a sense of competing styles will help you to fashion your own written voice.

The Simplest Word Choice

If you're stuck combing your mind for the right word, there are any number of "describer's dictionaries" available that might lead you to *le mot juste*. Or if not, such dictionaries will give you more adjectives detailing the nuances of a flower, for example, than you can imagine. But artful phrases (especially if they're French) can just as often distract readers from the simple word said beautifully. And a specialized vocabulary also stretches the bounds of believability. Unless your character is a florist, is there any reason she would use the word "marguerite" to describe a daisy?

For these reasons, Hemingway distrusted writers who overly relied upon a dictionary. Papa's dislike of the obscure word made for a famous exchange between our writer of the sparse style and the writer of the verbose sentence, William Faulkner. Faulkner had beaten Hemingway to the Nobel Prize by five years. In comparing their writing styles, Faulkner quipped: "He has never been known to use a word that might send a reader to the dictionary." There's much truth in Faulkner's statement. Hemingway did not think of successful writing as that which caused a reader to put down a story, pick up a dictionary to locate a musty word, and then return—interruption over—to the emotions that the story was trying to build. Hemingway responded: "Poor Faulkner. Does he really think big emotions come from big words?"[46]

Hemingway's preference for basic words is essential to his descriptive writing style. Writers should choose the "true" description over the artful one. The simplest word often sounds truest to a reader's experience. The recondite word—Get thee to a dictionary!—distracts from the summoned experience by dwelling on language that's artificial. Hemingway once suggested that any writer worthy of the job shouldn't depend on a dictionary. Read a dictionary three times over, he said, front to back, and then get rid of it.

By setting his novels in locales foreign to an American audience, however, Hemingway could use words that were exotic to the common ear. Papa used specialized vocabulary most often when describing the techniques of a sport. The word "sobrepuerta," for instance, translates only as "lintel" from a basic Spanish dictionary. Hemingway used it in his fiction as a special reference to a seating section of the Pamplona stadium, specifically the seats that overlooked the entrance gate to the ring.

Why this exception for foreign or professional vocabularies? For one reason, such words show the familiarity of an aficionado, if not a practitioner. More importantly, they are also appropriate in the context of writing about the sport. They carry the certain truth of experience rather than the flamboyance of a dictionary. In this way a safari hunter knows that "buff" refers to buffalo, best shot in the nose in order to avoid its horns deflecting a bullet. A fisherman knows that "drag" refers to a reel's resistance against the line as a fish pulls on it. A matador knows that "media-veronica" refers to cutting short a bull's charge.

Hemingway's lesson to the aspiring writer, then, is to use the simplest words that carry the sense of a description to the most people.

The Seldom Simile

Like alliteration or obscure word choice, Papa thought that writing should seldom rely upon maneuvers such as metaphors and similes, figures of speech that compare two unlike things.

The simile has, of course, been widely used throughout literary history. Chaucer compared the Lady White's beauty to being "like a torch," spreading its flame to all men's lanterns to see her without diminishing her comeliness. Stephen Crane's *The Red Badge of Courage*, a novel that Papa admired, describes a young girl as standing "like an undaunted statue" (although it's unclear if Crane himself wrote that phrase or if an editor later added it). Writers such as Henry James could extend a metaphor over several pages or an entire novel, as in *The Golden Bowl*. These turns of phrase do ignite something of the reader's imagination, sparking a sense of men consumed by a woman's beauty or the stony firmness of a girl's posture. Chaucer's simile resorts to a double abstraction, comparing a woman's beauty first to a torch and then to its fire spreading among many men's wicks.

Contrary to popular opinion, Hemingway did use similes in his writing. When he did they were typically brief, coming to a point quickly. And his similes were closer to Crane's style of a comparison to concrete objects, rather than the extended images of James or Chaucer. The title "Hills Like White Elephants" points to the central simile of an arguing couple. But that comparison of hills to elephants came amid idle chatter—meaning nothing as the couple avoids talking about their pregnancy. In *The Sun Also Rises*, Jake meets his friends when the town is preparing for the start of a fiesta, and he describes the café "like a battleship stripped for action."[47] The deep scars across Santiago's face in *The Old Man and the Sea* are described "as old as erosions in a fishless desert."[48] Papa could also use similes ironically, often to humorous effect. Perhaps his most famous ironic comparison involved Lady Brett Ashley, who had "curves like the hull of a racing yacht." This is to say no curves at all, but built for speed.

Beginning writers will often overuse similes that have become worn out: "sly like a fox," "blind as a bat," "strong like an ox." Such turns of phrase have more fizzle than flare. It may be that in a world of foxes, bats, and oxen, these phrases once carried concrete meaning. Now, they just litter up the language as cheap filler phrases. Such clichés have been used so often, in so many different contexts, that they've lost their potency. And like anything else of value, the more you have of a thing, the less valuable any one becomes.

The threadbare phrase also frequently appears in bad descriptive writing. The epitome of this is found with the sentence, "It was a dark and stormy night." Originally penned by Edward Bulwer-Lytton in 1830, that sentence has become the trademark of a style of writing that Hemingway hated most. Forget such florid writing. Overwrought and unnecessarily artful, such description is not only cliché but also emphasizes an artificial atmosphere over a touchable reality. If you find yourself indulging in description that echoes too well with what you've read—your nights are always "black as pitch," your woods always dark, always lovely, always deep—go back to observing the world rather than reading about it.

Exercise: Cut It Out and Cut It Down

The descriptive phrases below are overly flamboyant and rely upon over-the-top imagery. Try your hand at cutting out the unnecessarily gaudy with a description of quick, hard reality.

Example: "Roiling up a moment of resplendent mockery, her unintentional laughter cut into his manhood like a dart misthrown into cheap drywall."
Rewrite: "Not meaning to, she laughed. And before she could hold the laughter back, it hurt him."

1. His anger slowly diminished, like a stiff drink with too much ice sitting in the sun for too long.
2. Her green eyes smoldered like a building summer Caribbean storm, brewing out in the Atlantic before it crashed into land.
3. Her face turned white as a coral reef, bleached at the rising temperatures of an affair exposed for too long.
4. She heard him only in spurts, like a static-filled radio needing its antenna adjusted each minute.

What's the Point? Hemingway emphasized the true description, not the artful one. In learning to cut though the unnecessary, you should emphasize the reality of your fictional world. Not its stylistic tricks. (But if you find your prose too purple, you might consider a career as a pulp crime novelist.)

Mimicking Hemingway: Trimming Down a Story

In only seven paragraphs, Hemingway's "A Very Short Story" tells of an Italian-born love affair that ends in gonorrheal bathos. Beginning with one of the earlier iceberg exercises from this chapter, try writing a story that doesn't go over 500 words. When you're done, cut out 100 words. Follow Hemingway's principle of privileging one true word over dozens of flamboyant ones. Once there, can you cut out another 100 words? Writing as a minimalist means making each word you use count the most. If you like the tightness of this small story, you might use it as a launching point as we work in future chapters on character and dialogue, description and narrative.

Transforming a Writer into Papa

Hemingway's first novel was *The Torrents of Spring* (1926), a parody of *Dark Laughter* that ridiculed Sherwood Anderson's writing style. Hemingway borrowed the title from the novel *Spring Torrents* by Ivan Turgenev (which Turgenev took from a ballad). In writing it, Hemingway also referenced writers such as Mark Twain when his characters "light out for the Territory." Such a blend of imitations most likely allowed Hemingway to work through the stylistic influences of those he both detested and admired. What emerged next was a novel definitively in his own style.

Select a sentence from a writer whose style differs greatly from Hemingway: Henry James, Edith Wharton, or Jane Austen. Maybe William Faulkner, F. Scott Fitzgerald, or Zora Neale Hurston. As we've done with Poe's writing previously, try keeping the sense of this passage, but rewrite it in order to transform the voice into Hemingway's style. If you follow the key characteristics of the "lean, well-hewn" passage, can you make it seem as if Papa himself wrote this sentence?

Tracing Papa's Influences

Another way of seeing the qualities that make up Hemingway's style is to see what aspects of it have influenced other writers. Places to start? Try Cormac McCarthy's *Blood Meridian* (1985). Or check out Raymond Carver's short story collection *What We Talk about When We Talk about Love* (1988), Chuck Palahniuk's *Choke* (2001), or Amy Hempel's "miniaturist" style in *The Dog of the Marriage* (2005). Each of these writers has his or her own subject matter and identifiable style, but each also bears the recognizable echoes of the Hemingway sentence. Going down our list of the key characteristics of what makes up Papa's voice (omission, short sentences, repetition, etc.), how many can you find in a passage from one of these other writers? Now, pick a paragraph of this Hemingway-influenced style and rewrite it as we did with the earlier embellishment exercises. Add adjectives or stylistic flourishes that aren't there. Add details that you imagine the writer might have had in mind, but chose to leave out. By adding the inessential to what's already been published, you should be able to pick up a sense of why the minimum sets the style and rhythm to the Hemingway voice.

An *Immovable Life*:
The Forging of a Character

3

"*Now watch one thing. In the 3rd volume don't let yourself slip and get any perfect characters in . . . Keep them people, people, people, and don't let them get to be symbols.*"

(Hemingway, Letter to John Dos Passos[50])

For all of the effort a writer goes through to fashion a distinctive style or to provide realistic description, what readers often remember most from a story are its characters. When the fiesta's over and the story is told, characters are what linger most in a reader's mind.

Assembling a cast of what Hemingway thought of as "people" (not mere "characters") is one of the first challenges that any writer faces. Once these characters are drawn believably, however, other elements of a story will often come naturally from those personalities populating its pages.

Most writers over the course of their careers tend to write about a host of characters. But Hemingway spent much of his life writing and rewriting just one. He was called Nick Adams or Jake Barnes, Frederic Henry or Harry Morgan, Robert Wilson or Robert Jordan. He was a type of character that persisted through tales of youth and disillusionment, love and loss, hunting and war.

Because he drew his characters from breathing models, Hemingway's sketch of this recurring character also presented some version of himself to the world. Myths about Hemingway-the-writer sprung from his character as quickly as his stories rose in popularity. People speculated, wrongly, that Papa was a writer who had been made impotent by the war, as Jake Barnes had, or whose love for a nurse ended in tragic childbirth, as Frederic Henry's did.

It would be a mistake, however, to presume that this Hemingway hero appears and reappears in the same form from story to story. Each time he appears he carries a different motivation; a different conflict drives him. The obstacles in his way are unique each time he sets out: Jake Barnes's hopeless love against the bodily desires of Brett Ashley, Frederic Henry's torn duties to a war and to the pregnant Catherine Barkley, or Robert

Jordan's commitment to revolution diminished amidst the realities of wartime politics.

What unites these Hemingway characters into one type is something that literary critics have taken to calling the "code," the stoic principles of how the hero should react to the world around him. Presented with danger, he stands emotionally unshaken, a life immovable when threatened by either death or disaster.

Papa Says Hemingway coined the phrase "grace under pressure" in a letter to F. Scott Fitzgerald, describing the special qualities of a matador before the bull.[51] The phrase easily applies to many of Papa's "code heroes."

In this chapter, we'll work through what makes for believable characters, and characters that are interesting enough to read about. As Hemingway thought of them, writers should present characters as whole and complete people (including all of their flaws) and not as the grotesque caricatures that inhabit so much fiction. We'll look at how Hemingway drew inspiration for his characters and forged them into life. We'll look at the role the "code hero" played in how Papa thought about character motivation and conflict. Finally, we'll look at one of Hemingway's most enigmatic characters for how she went from the real-life Lady Duff Twysden to the fictional Lady Brett Ashley.

The Reality of Characterization: Where Papa Found Inspiration for His Characters

Hemingway's most often quoted comment on the invention of a character comes from *Death in the Afternoon*. In the rich paragraph that also provides his descriptions on style as architecture and on the Iceberg Theory, Hemingway wrote:

> *"When writing a novel a writer should create living people; people not characters. A character is a caricature . . . People in a novel, not skillfully constructed characters, must be projected from the writer's assimilated experience, from his knowledge, from his head, from his heart and from all there is of him. If he ever has luck as well as seriousness and gets them out entire they will have more than one dimension and they will last a long time."*[52]

Hemingway divided literary characters into two types, the caricatures of cheap imitation and the people of complex dimension.

Caricatures result when writers mistakenly see their work as the product of pure imagination, disconnected from the world in which they live. Notice that Papa dismisses unrealistic characters no matter how artistically a writer has crafted them. The successful writer, then, gets people into the pages of a story by looking to the world first and inventing through imagination afterward.

To become a skilled writer after Hemingway's example means having both a sketch artist's ability for observation and a psychologist's ability to understand human personality. Such open-mindedness may seem unlikely coming from the likes of Hemingway, a man who expressed strong, often slashing opinions of those around him. The quality of other authors' work often drew quick, summary judgment. But Hemingway distinguished between the need for an individual to render judgments about the world and the need for a writer to see people's motives. In order to create believable and realistic characters, a writer must understand how and why people do what they do.

Facts of Hemingway Papa thought little of one character: Joe McCarthy, the US Senator obsessed with ferreting out communist sympathizers in Hollywood and the American government and military. Living in Castro's Cuba, Hemingway wrote a letter that invited McCarthy to La Finca Vigía, all expenses paid. Instead of running his mouth for publicity, the senator could get out his frustration by fighting an old writer who at fifty years old would still beat him squarely. Besides, Papa thought, the beating might do McCarthy some good.

The Journalist's Eye

It's not difficult to see that Hemingway's beginnings as a newspaper reporter influenced his ideas about characterization. Papa's first stories came from Kansas City streets. Whether waiting at the police station, city hospital, or train station, Hemingway scoured the people of Kansas City for stories interesting enough to tell. Even someone easily overlooked, say an office messenger boy, might make a compelling enough character if he could land a strong right hook. By contrast, the ivy-league-educated minds of Scott Fitzgerald, Ezra Pound, and T.S. Eliot learned to tell their stories from the literature of ages lost. Fitzgerald had fashioned *The Great Gatsby* as a model of the Jazz Age, but a character such as Nick Carraway carried as much influence from Joseph Conrad's Marlow as he did from the author's own experience. Pound steadily turned toward the Greeks and the Renaissance. Eliot obsessed over tradition.

Aiming for realism, though, doesn't mean that you should incorporate any and all of the special ticks that set a character apart. Doing so would create a grotesque bundle of eccentricities, not a believable and consistent character. You should draw upon your sense of balance and selectivity in deciding what a scene should indicate about your characters.

Becoming a keen and patient observer of people is essential to Hemingway's techniques of characterization. Papa satirized the writer who too casually incorporated any person he may have witnessed. In *To Have and Have Not*, for example, Richard Gordon sees a large woman, bleach-blonde hair under a man's hat, crying as she passes by. Gordon sets out that night to write her into his political novel. His imagination fits the woman's tears neatly into his political agenda by making her husband, the strike organizer who despises her, the cause of her distress. But this presumptuous sketch is patently wrong. Unknown to Gordon, the woman is the wife of the novel's central character, Harry Morgan. She was crying because she had learned of her husband's death.[53] Gordon gets it wrong because as a writer he's more interested in conforming his characters to a political idea than in any serious understanding of people and their lives.

Writers who match people to some preconceived literary idea see only that idea, not complexity of character. Hemingway blasted John Dos Passos for this habit, turning characters into pawns in a game of political chess, the moves already planned out. Should the writer find a character too perfectly fitting into some artistic ideal, he should remember all the contradictions of human personality. Good people lie. Liars can be the most kind. The dying can feel most alive.

The Forging of Characterization: How Hemingway Invented His Characters

Hemingway's emphasis on people over caricatures in his fiction does not mean that his novels were a simple name change away from nonfiction.

When critics pressed Hemingway on the similarity of his characters to actual people, he was often annoyed with the suggestion that his skills as a writer were limited to those of the copyist. He was quick to defend novels such as *The Sun Also Rises* and *A Farewell to Arms* as pure acts of artistic imagination drawn from realistic characters.

But any emphasis on realism in character creation must also have an equal part invention.

While Papa always privileged people as the core of effective characterization, in reality he also drew upon the characters of other literary works for the models he used in his stories. The boy narrator of "My Old Man," as one example, bears a striking resemblance to similar characters from Mark Twain, Sherwood Anderson, or Ring Lardner. And of course, the literature that Hemingway read also directed where Papa went and filtered how he saw people, as in *The Dark Forest*'s influence on his entering the First World War. He satirized this role of literary desire in *The Sun Also Rises* when Jake Barnes tells Cohn that he'd want to go Africa if only he read a love story set there.

Papa Says The names of the central characters in *A Farewell to Arms* were adapted from Barklie Henry, a Hemingway friend whose wife had gone through a difficult labor.[54] When asked how he named his characters, Papa replied, "The best I can."[55]

Hemingway thought of himself as always in competition with other writers, so when he drew upon literary influences it was often to prove he could do it better. There was no use repeating what someone else had already accomplished. The key to Hemingway's freshness, then, came from both the radical style he developed and his ability to forge characters from those around him.

Inspiration Is Everywhere

Many of his characters were drawn from Papa's own experience, but he also fashioned characters from composite sketches of what he observed, what he read, and other people's experiences. In World War I hospitals, he listened to the stories of other wounded soldiers to give a depth to Frederic Henry that went beyond his own wartime experience. In characterizing Lady Brett Ashley, he grounded her in Lady Duff Twysden but also included in her portrait aspects of his wife Hadley. During the Pamplona fiesta, Hadley had been honored with a bull's ear by the famous matador Juan Belmonte. Hadley wrapped the ear in a handkerchief and placed in it a drawer, a detail that Hemingway included in characterizing Brett. As the unrealized love who met Jake in a war hospital, Brett also includes shades of Agnes von Kurowsky.

While Hemingway emphasized the importance of people over caricatures in fiction, he drew inspiration for the fictional people he created from the combined experiences of both real people and literary models alike. The lesson for the writer is to take inspiration where you find it and avoid abstraction. The practice of writing is to forge those inspirations into a character that works within the pages of a story.

Exercise: Characters out of People

Select two or three of the most interesting people that you know, perhaps for their personality, their family, or their profession. For each, make a list of the details that make that person interesting, perhaps personality traits or scenes that you've witnessed. Are there contradictions that make them stand out? Perhaps a dedication to a profession (art, medicine, law) but indulgence in an inhibiting addiction (drugs, lovers, television)? Now, following Papa's principle of the Iceberg Theory, select only the two or three scenes that you think might be needed to tell a story about this person. If you're lacking detail, you might extrapolate from what you know or combine similar details from other people into a composite list. But cross out any details that aren't essential.

What's the Point? Hemingway took his inspiration for his characters from listening to the people around him. To begin seeing which habits of people might make them an interesting character, it's useful to start looking for your fictional characters among family and friends.

Of Character and Papa's "Code"

Taking your inspiration from your own experiences and listening to those around you, how do you shape those observations into a believable character? As an aspect of a story—part of plot, setting, and point of view—what is a character?

F. Scott Fitzgerald once wrote, in the scrawled out story ideas of his notebooks, "Action is character."[56] He meant, in part, that what characters do is key to understanding who they are. He also meant that the action of a story (its plot) should follow from its characters and their conflicted interests.

But in the letters between them, Hemingway reprimanded Fitzgerald for using characters that departed from real-life models. You can't begin to model a character on a person and then change that person's background, parents, or education, he thought. Hemingway's ideas about character creation came from looking at what people had done in the past and inventing an imagined future around them. The writer's job was to invent from his past experience in such a way that his fictions could come true in a believable future. Storyteller, in this way, becomes fortune teller. But for both Fitzgerald and Hemingway writing in a modern moment, endless opportunities sprung into being for how characters might act in a new world of voting women and fast wealth, trench warfare, and government welfare.

Fitzgerald's notion that "Action is character," however, is as old as Aristotle, who defined character as both the outward actions taken and an internal ethical purpose that drives such action. This gives us a double meaning of "character": (1) the people of a story, your writerly representation of creatures that think and do, but also (2) the substance of moral principle, as in the phrase "moral character."

To understand how Hemingway created his characters and how he distinguished the "code hero" among them, it's important to see how these twin notions of "character" work. One operates above the surface, appearing in action and speech. The other most often lies beneath the surface, only hinted at in the behavior that appears on the page but fully developed in the writer's mind.

An external "character" that we can read about in print—or observe in the street—forms the basis for portraying believable people. It's the art of making characters seem like people we could meet in a café. This outside meaning of character includes the mannerisms and behavior that are an essential part of descriptive writing. It's an awareness of personality that leads to effective characterization.

The internal "character" of moral composition forms the basis of character depth, of conflict and complexity. It's the moral composition of the Hemingway "code hero"—for good or ill—that distinguishes this character type from all others. In *For Whom the Bell Tolls* (1940), Robert Jordan's willingness for self-sacrifice sets him apart from characters such as the disillusioned Pablo, unwilling to risk his life at war. This doesn't mean that the Hemingway "code hero" is necessarily a good person. The ethics of Jake Barnes and Harry Compton are rather problematic. But thinking of your characters as having complete, inner lives does suggest that they are more than what they appear to be on the page. Doing so makes them believable.

What defined this "code hero" to which Hemingway returned so often? Literary critics such as Philip Young saw in Hemingway's work a repeated type of hero, one who lived in a world with fleeting use for the masculine code by which the character gauged his own behavior. Nick Adams, Jake Barnes, Robert Wilson, Robert Jordan, Santiago, and many others fit the type. The "code hero" always suffers loss—in war, in the hunt, in love—but that was the way of any Hemingway story. What mattered was how the hero responded to such adversity. What mattered was how they distinguished themselves from other characters who surrendered under the same circumstances.

What gave the code heroes their inner lives was how they thought about and responded to that turmoil. Honor and dignity demanded that suffering be handled with grace. Thus, the "code hero" embodies both aspects of our definition of character: (1) the code suggests how characters can or should act, and (2) it suggests an inner standard (often unseen) used to judge those actions. There are certain behaviors that are acceptable and others that are not, as Jake Barnes knows, but the too-quick-to-cry Robert Cohn does not. The hero knew, out of manhood or out of morality, that submission resulted from breaking the "rules" of sport, as when Francis Macomber wants to shoot a lion from his car, or from cowardliness, as when Macomber bolts from the lion in the bush.

What Moves a Character: Motivation and Conflict

Most all of Hemingway's fictions are character-centered. Rather than a plot-heavy structure where stories revolve around the sequence of events (as in pulp thrillers), Hemingway's stories focus either on the motivations of an individual character or on the interchanges of several characters. Even Papa's nonfiction works such as *Death in the Afternoon* or *Green Hills of Africa* revolve around the Hemingway persona more than the action of any bullfight or safari.

In inventing characters for your stories, then, an important first step comes in understanding what compels them to act in the ways that they do. If action is character, character is also action.

Hemingway claimed not to have plotted out the events of a story beforehand. He claimed that he made up what would happen as it came along, based upon what the characters would do. To accomplish that successfully, you'll need a clear understanding of character motivations, which often exist at cross purposes to other characters or some event. When you're stuck on knowing where a story should go, return to your character's motivation and conflicts to decide what should happen next.

With one or two characters working against each other (with opposite motivations), your plots can spring into life. In "Hills Like White Elephants," for instance, the American man wants to be free from family, free from the seriousness of becoming a father. He wants his pregnant lover to have an abortion, telling her that their relationship will be unaffected afterward. The woman, while clearly undecided about whether to go through with the "simple operation," knows that it would forever change them. Either way, the happiness she wants is lost. Two characters plus opposing motivations over an unwanted pregnancy equal one classic Hemingway short story.

The idea of an actor asking, "What's my motivation in this scene?" has likely become a cliché. Yet, it's useful to think about characters as more than a simple series of dialogue lines. Actors want to know the psychology of their characters in order to make their performances believable, a type of the "iceberg principle" applied to the stage.

Writing fictional characters, then, means coming to understand not just one character (as an actor must) but all of the characters in your story. In "Monologue to the Maestro," Hemingway counseled that aspiring writers need to "get in somebody else's head for a change."[57] The examples that he gave with this advice all have to do with arguments, two or more people cursing each other out. It's not enough to judge who is right, who wrong. You should try to understand each person's reasons for lashing out at the other. You should try to understand how a person feels taking someone else's abuse.

Understanding a character's motivation means knowing what he wants. What goal does the character have? Is it to prove himself as a soldier? A fisherman? A man? Is it to win the love of a woman? To win her in bed? Your characters don't explicitly need to know their own goals. It's often more interesting when they don't. (How many of us know what we really want or how to go about getting it?) But you as the writer—knowing what lurks beneath the iceberg's surface—need to understand what those goals are as you portray them and throw them into a plot.

It's not enough for your characters to want something. A story about a man who wants a fish and buys one at the super-market is no story at all. But an aging fisherman, desperate to prove he can still play the old sport, who captures an enormous marlin, only to have it eaten away bit by bit while coming into port, has a story worth telling. The difference between stories that need to be told and those better left unwritten lies in con-flict, the struggle between what your characters want and the forces in their way of getting it.

Drama comes from obstacles to what your characters want. For Jake Barnes that obstacle is the impotence that won't allow him to pursue either romantic or physical love with Brett Ashley. Frederic Henry's obstacle is modern warfare that doesn't per-mit chivalric heroism for an ambulance driver. Obstacles can be other characters too, as Robert Cohn is to Barnes. Or, obstacles can be an internal part of characterization. Barnes, for instance, tortures himself by introducing Brett to Romero, a way of get-ting back at Cohn but also blocking his own desires for her.

Exercise: Desire and Denial in Character

Motivation gives your character a reason to act, to participate in the action of the story you're writing. Readers are likely to identify with those goals, if not cheering for your character directly, at least in being pulled along to see whether or not her desires are satisfied. Hemingway understood that drama was struggle, however, and any compelling narrative had to deny its characters' wants—to provide the tensions that make for an engaging story. Think of three Hemingway characters that you're familiar with, perhaps from three different stories. Can you identify what those characters' desires are? Why those wants are denied over the course of the narrative?

1. Character/Story	2. Desire	3. Denial
Jake Barnes, *The Sun Also Rises*	To appreciate Romero's bullfighting career	Brett seduces Romero

What's the Point? Characters' desires are a necessary element in the dimensions that make them people, not caricatures. By recognizing the obstacles faced by Hemingway's characters—and seeing that fully drawn, central characters often have complex and multiple conflicts—you should begin to develop a sense of what makes them so engaging.

A Character in Profile

When Hemingway began writing *The Sun Also Rises*, Brett Ashley's biography made up a great deal of the opening section. Hemingway struck out most of this backstory in the published version, but the fact that he wrote it grounded him with a sense of the fictional character he was building.

The Brett backstory closely mimicked the biography of Lady Duff Twysden, and Hemingway often joked halfheartedly about libel lawyers coming after him due to his characters. Writing this background information gave Papa a sense of his character's story, even if it never appeared in the finished novel. Consider it the unseen iceberg of character creation: it exists only in the writer's mind but allows a richer portrayal of characters on the page.

In creating characters, both from real-life models and those parts you invent, you'll find it useful to know something of their history before they even appear in your story. You should certainly have this sense of all the central characters in your story, and the important supporting ones too.

Exercise: A Character Dossier

Complete the following dossier to establish a quick profile of your character. You might begin by truthfully filling out the dossier with facts related to the real person on whom you're basing your character, perhaps one of those interesting people you picked out in our earlier exercise. But, libel lawyers awaiting, change the details enough to fictionalize the character to your interests.

Name:

Would or would not step into a ring with a bull (literal or metaphorical):

Favorite drink:

Favorite sport:

Body looks like:

"Has curves like a": _____

Walks like:

Voice sounds like:

Face looks like:

Hands feel like:

Lips taste like:

Breath smells like:

Clothes typically worn:

Ethnicity:

Date of birth:

Place of birth:

Currently lives in:

Typical mood at home:

Parents' names:

Parents' occupations:

Siblings' names and occupations:

Friends' names and occupations:

Rivals' names and occupations:

Person most likely to get into a fight with:

Education:

What he or she wanted to be when grown up:

First job:

Current job:

Typical mood at work:

Spends the most money on:

Favorite hangout:

(cont.)

Most frequent hangout:

Typical mood when out:

Crime most likely to commit:

Political ideas:

Religious ideas:

Ideal tourist destination:

Last tourist destination:

Greatest accomplishment:

Biggest tragedy so far:

Tragedy most feared to happen:

Takes pride in doing:

Feels shame in doing:

Believes people should do what to abide by their "code":

Detests people who do what in breaking their "code":

Strongest prejudice:

Favorite curse:

Best compliment given:

Most annoying habit:

Most endearing habit:

Virginity lost in what manner:

Sex life:

Typical mood after sex:

Principal goal:

Biggest obstacle:

What's the Point? In researching a character's background (or inventing it), you'll have a greater sense of the people inhabiting your stories. While you won't use all or most of these details in your story (and certainly not for all characters), a character background gives you a richer sense in framing what you will include. If you're having difficulty finding characters, try completing a profile for any of Papa's. Then, move on to the characters in your own life.

Exercise: Character Backstory

Now, based upon a character dossier you've completed above, write a two-to-three page fictional biography. For variation, you might try writing it in an objective encyclopedia-style fashion, then again as an autobiography in the character's own voice. As you develop a cast of characters, you might write a third version from the point of view of one of the secondary characters.

What's the Point? The idea is to develop a rich enough sense of the character that you can write convincingly about her in the scenes where she'll appear. When you start a story with your character in it, leave this biography aside. While you might allude to some of these backstory events in your narrative, most all of it should make up the unseen iceberg.

The Cast of Characters

While conflict is a concept best understood as happening within a character, there are also the conflicts that go on between characters. Most stories, of course, have a range of characters, some working together and others working against each other. But not all characters are equally interesting or equally important to the story.

Democracy may be fine in politics. But in the pages of a short story or novel, there is often a clear hierarchy among characters.

The Primary Character: A Protagonist

Primary characters are those most central to a story, most often the hero or antihero of a given tale. Because of the repeated appearance of the "code hero," Hemingway often has one character, always a man, who decides how the world should be. This character's conflicts—what he needs and what prevents him from getting it—are what fuel the action of the story. As the plot unfolds, readers are first pointed toward the "code" character to make sense of the narrative.

Even when you're not using the "code hero," your stories will likely have one character that's most important. This character is known as the "protagonist," the one without whom there would be no story.

The Greek word "agon" means "a struggle" or "a contest for a prize." The prot*agon*ist in a story, then, is the first character that readers identify with as he or she struggles through a story's obstacles. ("Prot-" carries the meaning of "before" or "that which gives rise to.") Appropriate for tragedies, "agon" also gives us the English word "agony." This sense suggests the suffering or anxiety the main character must go through in order to resolve a conflict, to achieve a desire. The hero's role in a narrative is to suffer.

While all protagonists are defined through the conflicts they face in a story, Hemingway's distinctive "code hero" was defined by the competition between his expectations of manhood and sport, womanhood and love, and the realities of a changing world. Jake Barnes's frustrated desires for Brett are set against the freed desires she represents as a "New Woman." Barnes's appreciation for the rituals of the bullfight are set against the excesses of the modern fiesta.

A Secondary Character: Antagonist

The "antagonist" opposes the primary character, standing between the hero and what he desires. ("Ant-" means "opposing" or "of the same kind by applying opposite force.") Villains are the most obvious of antagonists in a story, actively working against what a hero is striving for, but any character so thinly drawn as to oppose the protagonist at any point quickly falls into the category of caricature. This can make for an exhilarating story in the pages of a comic book or in the plot-driven drama of a detective novel. Hemingway's emphasis on "people" and getting at the depth of character, however, calls for more complex antagonists.

In *The Sun Also Rises*, Robert Cohn is a quintessential Hemingway antagonist. His rivalry with Jake is apparent in the opening paragraphs of the novel, where Jake pronounces that he was always distrustful of forthright people and of Cohn's claim to a collegiate boxing title. Jake wants Brett physically, but his wartime injury makes an affair impossible. Cohn carries on in his place. Where Jake meets disappointment with the stoicism of the "code," Cohn erupts in outbursts of violence and frequent tears when his pursuit of Brett is dashed. Jake ritualistically follows the bullfights with all the wonderment of an aficionado, but Cohn has no interest, preferring to linger after a woman.

Facts of Hemingway Robert Cohn was based on Harold Loeb. After Loeb abandoned his lover, Kitty Cannell, for Duff Twysden, Hemingway assured Kitty that he was writing a book to exact revenge on the couple with Loeb cast as the villain.[58]

Although Hemingway might not have admitted it, Jake Barnes and Robert Cohn are alike in significant ways. Tennis partners, both Americans are living abroad in Paris, touring Europe. They are both writers, Jake a correspondent and Cohn a novelist. They desire the same woman. These may seem like superficial similarities, but antagonists are often mirror images of the central character. One or two changes in personality or incidents of fate and we would see how the protagonist might otherwise have turned out, often for the worse.

This balance of characterization between antagonist and protagonist is important because little differences create the large distinctions that make a main character unique. Jake's adherence to the masculine "code" is what sets him apart from Cohn in their loves of sport and women. His abandonment of that code by introducing Brett to Romero—mingling her fickleness with his artistry—lets loose the novel's crisis, an act of jealousy that brings him nearer Cohn's level.

But an antagonist does not necessarily need to be a person. It can be any force that opposes the main character. In *A Farewell to Arms*, Frederic Henry's antagonist is the war and the collapse of the Caporetto retreat more than it is any individual character. In *The Old Man and the Sea*, Santiago's adversary is youth and strength, represented in the power of the marlin, the sharks, and the sea.

Character Type A "foil" is any character who highlights the properties of another through contrast, much as Pablo's self-interest contrasts against Robert Jordan's self-sacrifice in *For Whom the Bell Tolls*. The term comes from a jewelers' practice of placing a sheet of shiny metal under a gem to highlight its sparkle.

When the principle antagonizing force is an abstraction, however, it's still the role of secondary characters to highlight the special characteristics of a primary character through their differences. Thus, Rinaldi's womanizing contrasts sharply with Henry's romantic attachment to one woman, Catherine. Santiago's old age is set against the youth of Manolin.

Exercise: Throwing Characters Against Each Other

With a sense of their competing desires, create a list of motives that might make the two characters in each instance below enter into a conflict:

1. A woman with a small child and a college student reaching the checkout line in a crowded supermarket at the same time.

2. A twenty-something man walking his dog past a house with an older person sitting on the porch.

3. A gas station attendant working his way through school and a teenager cruising in her new car.

4. An aspiring writer, eager to know how to be published, approaching Hemingway after he's read the poor reviews of *Across the River and into the Trees*.

What's the Point? By seeing how characters compete with each other, either as obstacles in each other's way or by chasing after the same goals, you'll be on your way to setting up the key components of the plots into which you put them.

write like *Hemingway*

How to Fill Up a Room: The Supporting Cast

Primary and secondary characters come to the foreground of a story because they occupy a special place in plot development. They confront each other over the climax at a story's height. But while two characters can fill up a scene, most stories require a supporting cast to fill out the action.

You'll occasionally hear supporting characters compared to furniture, fixtures like the glasses and chairs necessary for a bar scene. Don't believe it. Supporting characters can be as memorable as primary or secondary ones, but the role they play in a story places them in a less important position. What distinguishes them is what they're missing: a role in the central conflict of a story.

Lady Brett Ashley is among the most fascinating of Hemingway's characters, one that readers and literary critics have begun revisiting more than Jake or Cohn. We also see significant elements of Brett's character, filtered as it is through Jake's narration. As the love object of the novel's men, she moves from Mike to Cohn to Count Mippipopolous to Romero to Jake. It's debatable whether or not she's passed between these men or moves on her own liberated fancy, likely a combination of both, but her function in the narrative is to set Cohn and Jake against each other.

Desire and denial are what establish the primary characters of a plot. Brett has desires too. As she tells Jake near the end of the novel, she's looking for a good time with a nice, awful man. You'll notice, though, that Brett always gets what she wants. There's no obstacle between her wanting a man or a drink and then getting it. With no obstacle, no conflict, there's no drama. The supporting character is there to flesh out the world of the struggling.

In creating supporting characters, it's important to remember that they shouldn't pull readers away from the central drama of your story. Any fully developed character will have a story of her own that's worthy of being told. But not all characters in a story can be fully developed. And if you crowd a narrative with too many characters, too many conflicts or details, it quickly diminishes the power of any one.

On the Rocks or Out of Fizz:
Round and Flat Characters

Another useful concept in deciding how to create your characters comes from the novelist E. M. Forster in *Aspects of the Novel* (1927). Forster explained that the complexity of a character would determine whether it was "flat" (having one dimension) or "round" (having many dimensions).

Forster's ideas about "flat" and "round" have become shorthand for writers to classify characters in a story. A flat character can be contained in one sentence. A flat character is built around one consistent attribute, a personality with a singular dimension. Such a character can be both very important and play an interesting role within the story, but is always consistent and never surprising.

Brett Ashley, intriguing as she is, can be summed up in one sentence: "Brett Ashley enjoys herself at the expense of men." There are any number of questions we could ask about Brett: why does she get such pleasure in a string of men, a string of bars? Why are the men of the novel so captivated by her fickle charms? What was it about the "Lost Generation" that enabled this behavior? Any answer, though, must come back to that one sentence.

A round character, by contrast, has the unpredictability of living people. A round character refuses to be limited to one concept, one personality trait or set of behaviors. A round character will not be contained within a single sentence. Such a character is drawn with a complexity great enough to surprise readers with his actions, but at the same time is able to maintain believability.

Facts of Hemingway Hemingway's early title for *The Sun Also Rises* was *Fiesta*. In a letter to Fitzgerald, Papa joked that he was working on a novel set in Rhode Island, about a pregnant girl waiting in prison for murdering her mother. The title, *The Sun Also Rises*, came from her vision as the juice flows through the electric chair. Mocking melodrama aside, the novel's title came from Ecclesiastes 1:5.

Jake Barnes could not be summed up sincerely in one sentence. He desires Brett but can't have her physically. To make up for this, he sets her up with a series of other men. First, he introduces her to his rival, the womanizing Robert Cohn. Then, despite wanting to preserve the purity of the bullfight, he introduces the seducing woman to Pedro Romero, bringing their fiesta of San Fermin to a brawling collapse. His introduction of Brett and Romero is surprising—why would he torture himself this way? Corrupt the two passions of his life? But is it believable? Certainly. Something about Jake's past, his personality, his motivation makes such self-immolation consistent with who he is. A psychologically complex man, Jake Barnes.

How Papa Saw It

George Plimpton asked Hemingway if he thought about his characters in the way that Forster might have categorized them. Papa answered with a typical gruffness when faced with the looming ideas of a rival: "If you describe someone, it is flat, as a photograph is, and from my standpoint a failure. If you make him up from what you know, there should be all the dimensions."[59]

Papa's point was that in description you're seeing a character only from the outside, like the mechanical lens of a camera. A photograph captures one angle of a person in one moment of time. It doesn't tell you why that person is where she is or why she does what she does. It doesn't tell you what happens outside the camera's narrow viewfinder. It doesn't tell you motive. Fully developing a character (and building from "what you know") means drawing upon the insight that a writer must have in order to understand people. It means understanding a person's motivations. It means inhabiting your characters' personalities for awhile and bringing their cluster of habits and mannerisms to the page.

But not all characters within a story can be round. Having each character as complexly developed as the next diminishes the importance of the central characters, the protagonist, and antagonist.

As Hemingway used the word, flat meant failure. Flat characters came from a writer creating them out of false preconceptions, making them hollow shadows rather than real people. The writer who merely described characters from literary stock, using stilted dialogue or unrealistic stereotype, failed to present believable people. In writing to Bernard Berenson, Hemingway explained that the key to his character creation lay with its accuracy rather than its artificial beauty. "Sometimes I can make people because, as a writer, I have almost a perfect ear."[60] Listening to people gave Hemingway the ability to hear them in their complexity, not hearing only what the writer of flat caricatures wants to hear. Dialogue became a key element for making his characters seem alive, their speech arising from the grubby ink of a page. (For more on dialogue see Chapter 4.)

Forster, however, did not mean flat as an insult to a writer's talent. By describing a character as "lesser" he was not thinking of the style of characterization that a writer might use to make a character seem like a person. Instead, Forster's description of some characters as "flat" and others as "round" had to do with their importance to the plot of a story, whether they were central or supporting characters. It's telling of Papa's priorities as a writer that he focused on the difference between "flat" and "round" as relating to the techniques of characterization in a given scene, rather than how their complexity relates to their importance in the story hierarchy.

Shaken and Stirred: Dynamic vs. Static Characters

Another concept important to keep in mind while fashioning your characters is the extent to which they change over a story. A character that has some striking revelation, converts to a new way of thinking, or changes some habit is "dynamic." The inner life of a dynamic character changes due to his action or the events that occur in a story. The coming-of-age character is classically dynamic, as with Liz Coates's tearful revelation from giddy love to uncompassionate sex in "Up in Michigan."

A character that is the same person leaving the story as he was entering it, is "static." The inner life of a static character remains the same come hell or charging bull.

While the dynamic vs. static distinction may seem similar to describing a character as either flat or round, they are different. "Flat" and "round" refer to the *depth* with which a character is drawn in a given scene or throughout a given work; "dynamic" and "static" refer to the *length* of a character's path in the story and whether or not she changes course. Where "flat" and "round" are aspects of characterization, "dynamic" and "static" are aspects of plot, how a character relates to the action of a story. The two concepts are, of course, related, as any dynamic character is likely also to be round, given the complexity required to create believable characters who are able to transform before the reader.

When deciding whether your characters will be dynamic or static, it's important to ask how the events of your plot might change characters in different ways. In *A Farewell to Arms*, the wartime realities of the Caporetto retreat and his coming role as a father changes something drastically in Frederic Henry. An entire cast of characters who react passively to the world, forever bending the same to tragedy or triumph, seldom holds interest for readers.

Papa's Techniques for Characterization

"Characterization" refers to the methods by which a writer can introduce and profile a character to the readers of a story. Just as there's much more to our personalities than what our filed taxes can indicate, characters must have a life richer than what is described on the page. How you select what characters say or how they act on that page, however, are the techniques of characterization through which readers meet the people populating a story. If a character is a complete iceberg unto itself, the part seen by readers above the water is the characterization through which it appears in the story.

There are, broadly speaking, four ways in which you can give readers insight into a character. For convenience, we'll take all of our examples from the way Pedro Romero, a supporting but significant character, is presented in *The Sun Also Rises*.

1. Direct narration. Tell readers what they should know about the characters. In direct narration, you give readers the characters' description and background information. This suggests how readers should think of the characters you're presenting. You might think that direct description occurs most often at the beginning of a story or when introducing a character, but it should also take place throughout the story as a whole.

Jake Barnes dominates as the narrator throughout *The Sun Also Rises*, freely giving his opinion of the expatriate crowd. It's clear that Jake's fondness for the bullfight as an art colors his descriptions of Romero. He tells readers that Romero was "real," a matador of the old school that put his life at risk when facing the bull. And Jake's description of Brett watching Romero channels something of his performance's eroticism.

2. Action. Describe what characters do. How characters perform and react can be a powerful way of comparing their actions against characters' ideas about themselves and other characters' ideas about them. Habitual actions are also what make a character consistent, even if he's habitually inconsistent. And if he breaks with those habits, that's an effective way of showing change in a character.

The description of Romero's "purity of line" while dancing with the bull testifies to the bravery that Jake claims about him. But Romero is more than what Jake makes him out to be. In Romero's first scene with the Pamplona revelers, Jake mentions that he's sure he doesn't speak enough English to understand Mike's insults. When Romero joins Jake and Brett later for a drink, he confesses that he speaks English well and only hides it to protect his reputation as a *torero*. Romero's suaveness with the bull carries over to Brett. He joins her in bed, an act that sets off the jealous charging of Robert Cohn. As he performs in the ring, so Romero performs in the bedroom.

3. Conversation. Convey what characters say about themselves and what other characters say about them. Because speech is an act, conversation may be a subset of action, but in Hemingway it's a powerful enough technique on its own to deserve a separate category. We'll further discuss how conversation can reveal character in our chapter on dialogue, but it's worth noting here.

How the Pamplona revelers talk about Romero's performance during the bullfight establishes his skill in the ring, his reputation among spectators, and something about how they relate to him. After all, what a person says about another can explain quite a bit about the person speaking. In the following exchange, notice Mike's drunken nonchalance and Brett's striking appreciation for fashion: "I say," Mike said, "that Romero what'shisname is somebody. Am I wrong?" "Oh, isn't he lovely," Brett said. "And those green trousers."[61]

4. Thought. Explain what characters are thinking and feeling. Giving readers the internal thoughts and emotions of characters can set them apart from what other characters say or even how your narrator presents them.

Since it's Jake who narrates the novel, the most direct inner thoughts that Hemingway can present are his. Jake does tell us Romero's motivations and inner strength at facing the bull—or at least Jake's own imaginings about the bullfighter. When Romero is in the ring, not looking up to the crowded stands, Jake sees Romero linking the bullfight to his love for Brett: "Because he did not look up to ask if it pleased he did it all for himself inside, and it strengthened him, and yet he did it for her."[62]

Exercise: A Table of Characters

In *The Sun Also Rises*, scenes frequently take place in a fiesta bar. Jake, Robert, Brett, Mike, Bill, and later Pedro all come together over drinks and witty dialogue. Write a scene (two to three pages, or longer this time) where you set a number of characters either at a dinner table or in a bar, some social gathering place that brings together many of your characters at once. Perhaps they're celebrating a modern-day fiesta by tailgating outside a football stadium. Perhaps they're celebrating a friend's promotion at work. You might complete character profiles and backstories for one or two of these characters—protagonist and antagonist, most probably. Then, surround these central characters with a supporting cast (husbands and wives, friends and rivals, coworkers and acquaintances). What techniques of characterization (narration, action, dialogue, thought) can you incorporate that bring out the primary and secondary characters from the background?

What's the Point? Many writers use the group scene as a tried and true device for figuring out how their characters relate to each other. Along with varying the characterization techniques, you might experiment with putting different characters' motivations and obstacles in play at different times within the scene. Be careful, though, not to turn your cast into a crowd. If all characters seem equally important and are equally "round," readers will be overwhelmed.

How Lady Duff Twysden Became Lady Brett Ashley

Perhaps the most enigmatic of Hemingway's characters is Lady Brett Ashley, as central to *The Sun Also Rises* as the bullfight is to *Death in the Afternoon*. Brett draws Hemingway's male characters into an orbit of sexual desire and drunkenness that winds a trail from Paris to Pamplona. Readers of the novel, by turns, have found Brett equally alluring and alarming. As the object of the novel's desire, she genuinely brings out the worst in her cast of lovers. It's ultimately through her effects upon the novel's men that we finally come to understand Brett. Seeing Brett Ashley through the lovers who compete for her attention may seem an odd way of understanding a person, and such a technique of characterization doesn't represent the woman whom she was based on.

How did Hemingway invent such a captivating, if flawed, character?

The Starting Point

The woman that became the model for Lady Brett Ashley was born Mary Dorothy Smurthwaite. Her father had lived a successful, if undistinguished, life as a Yorkshire wine merchant, but it was a life that did not meet her maternal family's aristocratic leanings. When her parents separated, she took her mother's maiden name, Stirling. With a French education and summers attended by the servants of her grandmother's Scottish mansion, Dorothy was groomed for a successful society marriage. She had two that failed.

During the war, Dorothy had volunteered for the British Secret Service, a job that gave her regular exposure to servicemen younger than her first husband, Luttrell Byrom. After her marriage to Byrom ended in divorce, Dorothy ascended the heights of social grace by marrying Roger Twysden, a commander in the Royal Navy. Roger was a drunk, but his family was British nobility. In this marriage she reinvented herself as Lady Duff Twysden. And it was under this name, awaiting the finalization of her second divorce, that she met Hemingway in Montparnasse, 1925.

Her Left Bank circle remembered Duff Twysden as a captivating, if carousing, woman. She had all the breeding of the aristocracy, but all the bawdiness of the Jazz Age. She also had a body, as Hemingway described it, "built with curves like the hull of a racing yacht."[63] Hadley Hemingway remembered her laughter and as a woman unreserved about her sexuality. (She also admitted that Duff might have had an affair with her husband, although she later assured herself that they hadn't. Duff certainly captured his attention.) Harold Loeb remembered her laughter too, but idealized her with an airy romanticism, noting her beauty and grace while praising her simplicity.

Loeb became Hemingway's rival for Duff's attention during the Pamplona fiesta that inspired *The Sun Also Rises*. His near brawl with Hemingway in a café alley, which erupted after Papa had inserted himself into an argument between Loeb and Duff's cousin, became the basis for the fictional fight between Robert Cohn and Jake Barnes. In life, Hemingway cracked a joke as Loeb set aside his glasses and jacket. Both walked away before they came to blows. In the novel, Cohn lays Barnes out. The real punches landed, however, with Hemingway's characterization of Loeb as Cohn, a weepy villain sheepishly fawning after a woman. Loeb's counterpunch came in his memoir *The Way It Was* (1959), written to refute the way Hemingway had documented that Lost Generation summer. Still, in this fight of macho honor spurred on by a desire for Duff, Loeb credited Hemingway's "boyish" smile with disarming both of their tempers.[64]

From these Pamplona experiences surrounding the bull-fights and fiesta brawls, Hemingway drew Duff Twysden into Brett Ashley. The first drafts of the novel would be heavily revised by the time Charles Scribner's Sons brought the book to press. The earliest versions kept people's names the same as their real-life counterparts: Loeb and Twysden, but also Kitty Cannell (who was fictionalized as Frances Clyne) and Pat Guthrie (fictionalized as Mike Campbell). Fitzgerald had read over an early carbon copy and suggested some major changes, particularly to an introduction that contained the Brett Ashley back-story. Hemingway responded by entirely striking these opening pages of exposition, choosing instead to begin with Jake's comments on Cohn. By his Iceberg Theory of omission, Papa had centered a novel around a pack of male desires for Brett Ashley, but then cut out the introduction that set her character up, sending it below the page's surface.

Facts of Hemingway At the end of *The Sun Also Rises*, Brett Ashley can only wish to speed off with Jake to Madrid. Duff Twysden realized a lasting marriage in the Americas with her third husband, an artist named Clinton King.

A Test for Papa's Technique

After the novel began to sell, however, Max Perkins wrote to Hemingway asking if he would like to include the excised Brett material in a prologue for future printings. Perkins imagined that readers would need to be introduced to the novel as a new style of writing and also be able to ground their perceptions of its quixotic heroine. He admitted, though, that Brett Ashley's sudden appearance in Chapter III produced good effect.[65]

Hemingway rejected Perkins's suggestion—even the editor himself was unsure of it. He did so out of a sense that adding more on Brett's character would upset the balance of the novel's unity. Papa stood by his decision as a writer to keep the material out, even though some readers might want an extended description of the character who so drove Jake, Robert, and Mike. He had hoped for a long career with Scribner's, but explained that he couldn't go against his instincts only to please an editor's desire. If *The Sun Also Rises* didn't sell, maybe he could learn to write better books that would.

To understand Hemingway's complicated process of starting with real people and using them as a basis upon which to forge fictional characters, it's necessary to understand Papa's second reason for cutting out Brett's backstory. Those early draft sections were too close to a nonfiction fidelity to Duff's life. They weren't the literary inventions of a fiction writer. "That was the only stuff in the book," Hemingway wrote, "that was not imaginary—the Brett biography."[66] This distinction of Hemingway's between reality and fiction is important because it suggests how the writer thought of the creative work of character writing. Characters had to be believable as people, but in the end they were ultimately the products of fiction, not biographical sketches.

If Brett began with a real-life model but was ultimately summoned by Papa's imagination, were there other characters in literature that influenced her creation? Yes, although Papa protested that the answer was no. Hemingway had become quickly displeased when a critic complained that the novel stole Brett's characterization from the stories of Michael Arlen, an Armenian writer who had found success with *The Green Hat*. Hemingway maintained that he had never read Arlen's work. Besides, Hemingway claimed, he did not look for the models for his characters in fictions or any other idealized notions, be they romance, politics, or economics (despite what a study of his literary influences tells us). He found his models in the people he knew. He commented, ironically, "So now it is pretty amusing to have known a girl and drawn her so close to life that it makes me feel badly—except that I don't imagine she would ever read anything—and watch her go to hell completely—and assist at the depart," and then to have a critic claim she was stolen from another fiction.[67]

Habits of Hemingway If Hemingway rendered his fictional characters after real people, he also had a tendency to remember people through the fictions he read. Hemingway recalled Twysden confessing that her husband, Sir Roger, slept with a sword between them. As Hemingway's biographer Kenneth Lynn points out, though, that memory was almost certainly transplanted from Maurice Hewlett's novel *The Forest Lovers*, which Hemingway had read as a boy.

Brett as Composite

It would be a mistake, however, to think of Duff Twysden as the only source for Hemingway's characterization of Brett Ashley. There were plenty of women Hemingway knew who contributed aspects to Brett's character: Hadley had once been honored with a bull's ear after a bullfight, a prize she dutifully wrapped in a handkerchief and placed in a drawer. That scene made its way into *The Sun Also Rises* with Brett having the honor of the ear. Zelda Fitzgerald's excitement for late-night parties and her enjoyment in embarrassing Hemingway also showed up in Brett. Biographers who have psychoanalyzed Papa (a profession for which the writer held much contempt) have gone so far as to see in Brett echoes of Agnes von Kurowsky and even Grace Hall Hemingway, the writer's mother.

Hemingway's characterization of Brett Ashley may have started with the study of one real woman, Duff Twysden. But it should be apparent that Brett's fully developed character, as presented in the novel, was drawn as a composite sketch from observations of many women (and the influence of other literary characters). Hemingway chose the elements of Brett's character not out of a sense of faithfulness to his biographical model, but rather out of a sense of artistic creativity. In forming a rich character, he was able to establish the conflict between Jake and Cohn.

The characters that Hemingway forged in *The Sun Also Rises* so resonated with the novel's American audience that in the year following its publication a readers' cult sprang up on college campuses throughout the country. Dog-eared copies of the novel were read three or four times over. Debates—often enough drunken—sprang up amongst the undergraduate set over Hemingway's characters, his far-away cities. And while Papa created his characters from flesh-and-blood people, women of flesh and blood now fashioned themselves after the fictitious New Woman, Brett Ashley. A 1928 article in *Harper's*, suggesting that the young needed books that helped them "out of their confusion," condemned Hemingway's novel along with Joyce's *Ulysses* for their effects upon impressionable youth.[68] (That same edition ran another article comparing a woman's romantic role in society as a merchant in the "Marriage Market.") But with characters so suggestively drawn in Hemingway's iceberg style, the competing desires of Brett, Jake, and Robert came together to produce a novel that spoke to a generation of readers, each lost in their own way.

Exercise: A Composite Sketch

Hemingway drew Brett Ashley from a number of women that fit into the "type" of heroine she came to be. Go back to the first exercise of this chapter, "Characters out of People (page 87)." Look through those people that you initially found to be most interesting. If you've used one to begin sketching a character profile, look through your list for details from other characters that would add to a fully developed character. Don't be afraid to combine aspects of different people's personalities to create an interesting character.

What's the Point? While Hemingway said he created his characters from real life, bare reality can often be quite boring. And, egalitarianism aside, not all people are compelling enough on their own to form the basis of a story. Therefore, follow Papa's example in picking and choosing which aspects of a person are interesting enough to include. Your guiding principle should be one of believability, though. Remember that Hemingway dismissed writers who made characters from unrealistic circumstances or invented them out of abstractions such as politics or faith.

Mimicking Hemingway: Characters in Unrequited Love

Hemingway made a habit of using women he was in love with, or at least fascinated by, as the basis of his fictional characters. Duff Twysden as the model for Brett Ashley, Agnes von Kurowsky as Catherine Barkley. Often the women who rejected him or put off his advances became the stories' heroines.

Complete a fictionalized character profile based upon an early love interest of yours. Change enough details so that we couldn't identify him or her in a phonebook, but make it an accurate profile in history, personality, and appearance. Now, write a scene (two to three pages) based around this fictionalized old flame. Write about what you would have wanted to happen before the romance dwindled. A consummation? A fight? An explanation for why it never worked out? A bit of schadenfreude at how the lover ended up? This exercise can be cathartic. It's also one that might be treated delicately with any current lovers (although such delicacies never stopped Papa from writing about lingering desires for a not-so-old flame).

Characters after Love

As a man of four marriages, Hemingway also knew how to fall out of love and use that tension in his stories. "Hills Like White Elephants," "Out of Season," and "The Short Happy Life of Francis Macomber" all show couples quarrelling but still stuck with each other.

Complete character profiles for two former lovers who have fallen out because they desire different things—perhaps different families, careers, or newer lovers. Write a scene (two to three pages or so) with this couple in a situation where they can't get away from each other, perhaps on vacation or at a family gathering. Will they bring up what's been troubling them or just hint at it with darting comments? If you're following the Iceberg Theory, you might carefully select which elements of the conflict are essential to produce the tension between them and keep only those in your scene.

For the Love of Sport

Hemingway had a passion for sports that he channeled into his characters: Jake Barnes's love of bullfighting, Nick Adams's fondness for fishing or skiing, and Santiago's conversations about baseball. Often these characters proved their worth by showing their familiarity with the technical (if not artistic) nuances of the sport.

Create a character profile for someone who is either an athlete or aficionado of a modern-day sport. If you're not familiar with the sport, you'll need to do some research, and for Hemingway that means more doing than reading. What is it about the sport's technical aspects (a pitcher's throw, a fly fisherman's cast, a skier's carved turns) that satisfy or frustrate your character? Does your character do it for self-satisfaction? To escape something else that's troubling him (a traumatic event, a failed love)? For the reputation that being an athlete or sportsman brings him? Write an action scene (around two to three pages) where you show this character performing the motions of the sport (the windup, the flick of a wrist, the bend of the knees). Now, add some obstacle to this character's ability to enjoy the performance—old age and a younger competitor, some feat that's never been accomplished, a relationship or responsibility that gets in the way of the sport. For Nick in "Big Two-Hearted River" the obstacle to his fishing and reconciliation with his wartime past comes in the dark turn of the river into a swamp.

Dialogue: Or, Having Your *Characters* Do Things with Words

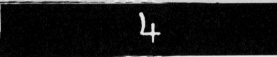

4

"It is in dialogue, almost entirely, that Mr. Hemingway tells his story and makes the people live and act."

(Conrad Aiken on *The Sun Also Rises*, 1926)

Dialogue refers to the conversations between characters, the moments in a story when one character says something aloud to another. The style of a dialogue can take as many forms as there are voices to be heard, but all good dialogue—whether used in fiction or creative nonfiction—remembers that it's taking place within a story. Hemingway kept this balance of believable voices and purposeful speech in mind throughout his writing. And if Papa's influence as a writer is most remembered for the sparse style of a sharp sentence, his characters are most remembered for fatalist quips over bulls, bullets, or hard drinks.

The art of a Hemingway dialogue, however, lies in subtlety and implication. For all of his reputation as the straight-talking, cut-to-the-chase maverick of American writing, Hemingway crafted his characters out of the indirect phrase. A review of *The Sun Also Rises* put it this way: "The characters are concisely indicated. Much of their inherent natures are left to be betrayed by their own speech, by their apparently aimless conversation among themselves."[69] As the novel's characters drink themselves through the malaise of modern Europe, their chic quips dangle meanings always implied but outwardly avoided. It would be a mistake, however, to think that Hemingway's scripted conversations are either aimless or arbitrary.

More than any other element in Hemingway's writing—plot, descriptive detail, setting—it's through dialogue that Hemingway establishes his characters and the dramatic tension between them. In this chapter, we'll examine how Papa scripted his short story "The Killers" almost entirely out of dialogue, focus on the strategies he used to make that dialogue come distinctly from his characters, and work on developing our own craft through a series of exercises that emphasize Papa's techniques.

Papa Says In an interview with *The Paris Review*, Hemingway claimed that Gertrude Stein "had learned to write dialogue from a book called *The Sun Also Rises*. I was very fond of her and thought it was splendid she had learned to write conversation. [. . .] She already wrote very well in other ways."[70]

Taking the time given him from a canceled bullfight, Hemingway wrote "The Killers" in one Madrid afternoon. And as Papa himself told George Plimpton, he completed two other stories that day, "Ten Indians" and "Today Is Friday." After first appearing in *Scribner's Magazine* in 1927, "The Killers" was subsequently republished in a number of Hemingway collections: *Men without Women* (1927), *The Fifth Column and the First Forty-Nine Stories* (1938), and *The Nick Adams Stories* (1972). Hemingway gave permission for the players at the Rand School of Social Science to adapt it into a play version, and the story has provided the basis of several films. A 1946 film *noir* version, staring Burt Lancaster and Ava Gardner, closely followed Papa's dialogue in its opening sequences. Reflecting on the film, Papa once commented that is was the only decent film adaptation ever done of his work. A later film version starred Lee Marvin, Angie Dickinson, and Ronald Reagan. Traces of the story's signature dialogue—gangsters arguing over diner etiquette—can be seen in other films such as *Reservoir Dogs* (1992) or *A History of Violence* (2005).

Dialogue and Its Importance to the Story

Dialogue can serve a number of purposes within a story: it can drive the dramatic tensions between characters, set up the suspense elements of a plot, or establish believable characters. And knowing when characters should speak in a story—in addition to what they should speak about and how they should say it—is an important skill for an effective dialogue writer to have. Hemingway's use of dialogue is so distinctive because of its powers of suggestion, such as a discussion between two characters about a bullfight that becomes a commentary on the sexual anxieties between them. The first step in understanding how Hemingway creates such tensions through dialogue is to see how those exchanges between characters are plotted within the story as a whole, from beginning to end. What purpose does a moment of dialogue serve at the opening of a story? At its climax? At its resolution?

To understand how Hemingway plotted specific moments of dialogue to serve the purposes of a story, let's examine how he orders certain conversations at key moments of the "The Killers," one of Papa's series of short stories that follows the Nick Adams character. In it, two assassins have come to the town of Summit, Illinois, to carry out a hit on a retired boxer, Ole Andreson.

Papa Says Giving advice on writing to Carol, his younger sister, Hemingway warned against using adjectives such as "swell" to cover up the laziness of not thinking up proper words. "Try and write straight English," Hemingway wrote, "never using slang except in Dialogue and then only when unavoidable."[71]

Very little happens in "The Killers" in terms of an action-driven plot. In fact, the story turns around two rather anticlimactic moments: first, the pair of murderers enters a diner to kill Andreson, "the Swede." But Andreson never shows up. In the second part of the story, Nick Adams flees the diner to warn Andreson that the hit is on. Here, we might expect a great *corrida* showdown between the Swede and his shotgun-bearing callers. Or perhaps the chase of hunters and hunted will begin. But neither happens. When Nick asks Andreson if the police should be warned or if he'll get out of town, the Swede only replies in defeat, explaining that he's done with fleeing. We leave him lying on his bed, facing a wall, awaiting his fate.

With a plot centered on such inaction, what, then, has made "The Killers" one of Hemingway's most popular Nick Adams stories? The total dominance that dialogue has over any other story element stands out most in "The Killers." Taking account of the text within quotation marks versus that not in quotation marks, we see that voiced exchanges between characters make up at least 90 percent of the ink on the page. The sparseness of narration in "The Killers" is made up for by the performance of a robust dialogue. Stories such as "Hills Like White Elephants" or "A Clean, Well-Lighted Place" also move readers quickly through extensive character exchanges.

Dialogue in "The Killers" can be broken down into five distinct Acts of exchanges. Just five moments of planned conversation take us from opening to (anti)climax to resolution:

I. Two hit men, Al and the rather garrulous Max, enter a diner. They argue with George, who works the counter, over the menu selection and the time of day.

II. Al and Max force Nick Adams (the only other customer present) into the kitchen with Sam the cook, tying them both up. Max jaws on with George about their plans: "I'll tell you . . . We're going to kill a Swede. Do you know a big Swede named Ole Andreson?"[72]

III. The evening passes as a series of customers come in for dinner, only to have George tell them that Sam's out. When Andreson doesn't appear, the hit men have to decide what to do with the witnesses to their planned crime. Max decides to leave them be, but Al complains, "It's sloppy. You talk too much."[73]

IV. With the hit men gone, Nick leaves to warn Andreson at his rooming house. Unwilling to flee and not wanting to tell the police, Andreson says, "There ain't anything to do. After a while I'll make up my mind to go out." In leaving, Nick talks with the rooming-house custodian, Mrs. Bell, about how gentle Andreson is. "He's an awfully nice man."[74]

V. In the story's coda, Nick returns to the diner and tells George of the Swede's reaction. Against George's fatalistic indifference, Nick responds, "I'm going to get out of this town . . . I can't stand to think about him waiting in the room and knowing he's going to get it."[75]

If asked to summarize "The Killers," most of us would likely say it's about two hit men out to find a retired boxer, or we might say it's about Nick Adams's coming of age in a moment of violence. Does that mean the dialogue exchanges of Act I—talk of menus and clocks—are idle chit-chat? Papa filling up the pages until we get to the thrill of Acts II and III? Not so.

Tension from Dialogue

The initial dialogue of Act I sets up the twin tensions that the story will resolve, beginning with the suspense over what will happen when Andreson walks through the diner door and into the waiting fate of the killers. In George's argument with Max over what time of day the dinner menu begins and a clock running twenty minutes too fast, Hemingway sets up the narrative tension around Andreson's expected 6 P.M. walk through the door. Readers must then count hours into minutes in Act III: 5:00, 5:20, 6:15, 6:20, 6:55, 7:00, 7:05, 7:10. The suspense effect at work here makes readers anticipate a forthcoming tragedy. Tension builds as we await Andreson's appearance. When he doesn't appear, the anticipation shifts to the fates of George, Nick, and Sam. Will they be murdered to cover up the hit men's plans? If Hemingway hadn't begun with George and Max's dialogue over a clock running twenty minutes too fast, the countdown of Act III may have seemed forced.

The other-than-casual conversation of Act I further establishes a second dramatic tension between the outsiders and the locals of Summit. In what seems like a banal discussion over whether Max can get chicken croquettes or must settle for bacon and eggs, Hemingway highlights the foreignness of two killers at a small-town lunch counter where everyone gathers to eat: "They all come here and eat the big dinner."[76] Al and Max don't know the customs. They're forcing their expectations on apple-pie America. By the story's last exchange, however, Nick himself resolves to leave town—to make himself an outsider—and flee from those willing to do nothing and simply take the injustice that life brings. This gives readers a resolution that makes the story seem whole: the awakening of Nick Adams to a world that's indifferent to violence. Andreson may accept the arrival of his fate in the guise of Al and Max, but Nick realizes that all Summit's citizens seem paralyzed with inaction, unable to stand up for an "awfully nice man." By beginning the story with a clash in dialogue between big-city outsiders and small-town locals, Hemingway is able to conclude the story convincingly with Nick and George's Act V conversation.

Exercise: The Arc of Dialogue

Select three Hemingway short stories and examine the dialogue that Papa uses to introduce his characters. Then, look at the story's closing moments of dialogue. Are there tensions raised by the opening dialogue that are then resolved in the closing dialogue? In what ways?

Papa's Tale	Opening Dialogue	Dramatic Tension	Closing Dialogue	Resolved Tension
"The Killers"	Al, Max, & George argue over menu: "That's the way you work it."	Outsiders vs. Insiders Violence vs. Inaction	Nick to George: "I'm going to get out of this town."	Nick can't stand Summit's acceptance of violence, so he becomes an outsider himself.

What's the Point? The purpose of this exercise is to understand how Papa's scripted dialogue functions as an element of plot—the purpose driving how a moment of dialogue is placed in the story.

How to Do Things with Dialogue (and Only Dialogue)

There's a curious plot element in Hemingway's "The Killers" that we have to question: why would George, Nick, and Sam do anything that Max and Al tell them to do? When Max orders Nick to join George and then Sam to come out from the kitchen, there's no description of the sound of Max's voice, menacing or otherwise. Nor are we told of any physical threat by Al and Max, who remain seated at the counter while ordering Nick around the counter. A gun? Hemingway doesn't directly describe Al's shotgun until just before he and Max leave the diner, its "cutoff barrels" making a "slight bulge" beneath a "too tight-fitting overcoat."[77] And we don't read that description until well after the hit men's demands have been followed, their taunts endured.

Why, then, do readers find it believable that Nick and Sam would allow Al to take them into the kitchen and tie them up? It's in the dialogue.

Reading the story to its end, we might backtrack and presume that Al's shotgun had been noticeable all along, if curiously unmentioned in the narration. Certainly the hit men's derby hats and black overcoats, their silk mufflers and gloves—described early in the story—suggest the stereotype of the mafia, particularly given the brashness with which Al and Max treat the Summit locals. But in reading the story from the beginning, it's through Al and Max's dialogue that Hemingway establishes the threat they pose along the way.

Hemingway's dialogue *suggests* much more than it *reveals*—another aspect of the Iceberg Theory that Papa explains in *Death in the Afternoon* (See Chapter 2). We don't need to have a shotgun described because the belligerent back-and-forth of Al and Max's rapport creates the same effect: intimidation. While all good writers use characters' speech in this way, what stands out in Hemingway's dialogue is its bareness. Hemingway's boldness lies in his trust of dialogue to carry a scene completely.

The style of dialogue used by other writers (including some that Papa deeply admired) can often be couched amid long passages of narration or description. In Dostoyevsky, where characters often "exclaim," "cry," or "pronounce," character dialogue etches the human out of religious, psychological, or philosophical abstractions. In *The U.S.A. Trilogy*, John Dos Passos—a friend Papa referred to as "Dos"—used the technique of having several characters voice their lines in one paragraph, typically without assigning given lines to specific characters. Dos Passos's "paragraph conversations" become a stylistic commentary on the sum of a conversation being more important than its parts, a style suited to his novels' social politics. With Hemingway, dialogue often appears with less ink on the page than the white space around it. Its nakedness suggests both character and scene.

Dialogue and Tone

Hemingway used dialogue in this suggestive manner throughout his career. In "The Killers," Al and Max's bullying and the threat of the shotgun yet unseen are suggested by their argument over a menu. In *The Sun Also Rises*, a conversation about bulls being unloaded in Pamplona suggests the sexual anxieties of Mike, Brett, and Cohn, the "ignored tensions" that explode during the fiesta. In "Hills Like White Elephants" a couple's indecision over a drink—*Anise del Toro*, with water or without—suggests their yet-unspoken argument about an abortion.

Habits of Hemingway Hemingway reporting to *The Paris Review* on the origin of "Hills Like White Elephants": "I met a girl in Prunier where I'd gone to eat oysters before lunch. I knew she'd had an abortion. I went over and we talked, not about that, but on the way home I thought of the story, skipped lunch, and spent that afternoon writing it."[78]

To see how Hemingway's dialogue accomplishes more than what's literally on the page, let's look at the conversation between Max, Al, and George just before the gangsters begin ordering townspeople about. Max and Al have just started eating their lunch, but Max isn't too sure about the glare George is giving them. How does Hemingway achieve the intimidation he needs out of Max and Al?

"What are *you* looking at?" *Max looked at George.*

"Nothing."
"The hell you were. You were looking at me."
"Maybe the boy meant it for a joke, Max," Al said.
George laughed.
"*You* don't have to laugh," Max said to him. "*You* don't have to laugh at all, see?"
"All right," said George.
"So he thinks it's all right." Max turned to Al. "He thinks it's all right. That's a good one."
"Oh, he's a thinker," Al said. They went on eating.[79]

If the sound of Joe Pesci's or Al Pacino's voice comes to mind when reading the above—maybe a scene out of *Goodfellas* or *Scarface*—there's good reason. The combative tones of the urban thug are unmistakable. But Hemingway wrote that dialogue before

James Cagney or Edward G. Robinson first brought the gangster voice alive in American movies.

The dialogue that Hemingway scripts in the above scene sets up the next one, when the hit men begin ordering George and Nick around. From the opening dialogue, readers know that Max and Al are argumentative and wildly out of place, but here we see the characters turn hostile to George, challenging him in a restaurant where he runs the counter. Hemingway first scripts a confrontation over George's casual look, and George quickly backs down from Max's challenging, "What are *you* looking at?" Already backpedaling, George quickly agrees to the gangsters' demands to stop laughing, "All right." Setting up the pattern of George's backpedaling makes the townspeople's submission to Al and Max believable. And this early confrontation sets up the anticipation that something drastic is about to happen, the mystery of why Max is implying that things aren't all right.

Notice, also, what's absent from the scene. For narration, we have only Max's look to George, George's laugh, and Max turning to Al. We're never told George's thoughts or given a physical description of his being afraid—no quaking in the knees, no breaking out in sweat, no voice trembling. Description? Nothing. Setting? Nada. The dialogue works, of course, because earlier paragraphs have shown Max and Al sitting in their overcoats, eating their dinner with gloves still on (and why are their gloves still on?). But once we get to the moment when the dialogue establishes the suspense for what's to come, the speech is almost entirely on its own.

Writing Believable Dialogue

Dialogue can be one of the most effective techniques in creating believable characters. A spoken line or two can convey more about a character's personality than can whole paragraphs of description. At the same time, awkward or stilted dialogue can quickly kill your readers' interest in the story. The key to writing believable dialogue, then, lies in balancing realism and good storytelling, both of which Hemingway excelled at.

To be realistic, dialogue should call to mind how flesh-and-blood people actually talk. In a fiction workshop, you'll often hear people refer to someone developing a good "writer's ear." They're describing someone attuned to the voices and rhythm of everyday speech.

To be good storytelling, written dialogue should always serve the purpose of the narrative. Effective dialogue cuts out the inessential. It should not be filled with meaningless jabberwocky. This is especially true in Hemingway dialogue. Papa's characters are most known for the short phrase, the quick quip. There's nothing longwinded or rambling in the couple's conversation in "Hills Like White Elephants": "I know you wouldn't mind it, Jig. It's really not anything. It's just to let the air in."[80] And when Hemingway's characters seem most aimless in their conversation, that's when they'll be most direct at revealing their anxieties. Dialogue should establish characterization, provide the plot, and elicit dramatic tension. Your characters shouldn't just talk to fill out a page—although they might in an early draft.

Writers on Papa "I have never understood, to this day, how Hemingway achieved his powerful dialogue . . . Hemingway offered . . . not dialogue overheard, but a concentrate of it, often made up of superficially insignificant elements—mere fragments of everyday phrases, which always managed to convey what was most important."[81] (Ilya Ehrenburg, Russian novelist)

Where did Hemingway spend his time listening, in order to pick up the voices used in "The Killers"? In his biography of the author, Kenneth S. Lynn points to Hemingway's direct experience with criminal low-life when he worked as a teenage reporter for the *Kansas City Star*, or his time hanging out at the Venice Cafe in Chicago, the prohibition "city of sin and sometimes gin." But Papa also tempered those life experiences with an eye toward good storytelling performance. Literary critics such as Ron Berman have pointed out that much of Al and Max's back-and-forth shtick comes from the style of the vaudeville comedy routine.

The Writer's Ear

What does Hemingway say about developing your "writer's ear"? In "Monologue to the Maestro," which was written in the genre of the dialogue between an aspiring youth and the man of letters, Hemingway offers the following: "Listen *now*. When people talk listen completely. Don't be thinking about what you're going to say. Most people never listen. Nor do they observe."[82] Papa meant that most of us plow through conversations waiting for another person's silence. Then, we jump in with whatever we want to say. When other people are speaking, we're thinking about what's going to come out of our mouths next. We're not observing what they say or how they say it. To create the powerful dialogue that propelled so much of Hemingway's fiction, you'll need to listen to the nuances of people's speech. You'll need to pick out the turns of phrase that typify people through their speech. Criticizing F. Scott Fitzgerald for what he saw as the flaws of *Tender Is the Night*, Hemingway wrote: "A long time ago you stopped listening except to the answers to your own questions. . . . That's what dries a writer up (we all dry up. That's no insult to you in person) not listening. That is where it all comes from. Seeing, listening. You see well enough. But you stop listening."[83]

Papa Says Hemingway on developing his own "writer's ear" from Ring Lardner: "Imitated Ring Lardner as a kid but didn't learn from him. Nothing to learn because he doesn't know anything. All he has is a good false ear and has been around."[84]

Listen, *now*. An essential technique toward crafting believable Hemingwayesque dialogue comes from training yourself to listen to the words and tones people use when they talk. Before we learn to listen to speech in this way, what typically stands out is the speaker's message. We're intent on hearing the information or purpose driving a statement or question, not the words themselves. When someone gives us directions, we listen typically for what roads to follow, what turns to take, what landmarks to look for. We're less likely to take account of the false starts and stutters that fill everyday talk—the *"uhs," "hmms," "well-you-know,"* and *"it's-sorta-like"* filler phrases that occupy the silence as most of us compose what we're going to say.

Not everything you hear, of course, belongs in written dialogue. Most of what we say makes for perfectly uninteresting literature. And a conversation pocked with strings of *"you knows"* quickly becomes tiresome. *Realistic dialogue does not mean actual speech.* It means dialogue that conjures believable sounds of speech in the mind of a reader. The artistic term for this idea is verisimilitude, which means giving the appearance of truth, not a simple transcription of reality. For this reason, Raymond Carver did not think that Hemingway's style of dialogue (nor his own) was a simple reproduction of people's speech. For Carver, the dialogue effect that Hemingway invented as an author—and those later writers who have since been influenced by him—came from a sense of rhythm and repetition. It did not simply reproduce the banal language of most daily conversation.

A useful exercise to train yourself in noticing the varieties of human speech is to listen to a talk radio show that allows people to call in and speak on-air. Radio hosts are professional broadcasters who are trained to use on-air time efficiently. Broadcast speech, then, is typically brief and as to-the-point as possible. This doesn't mean that broadcasters never use filler phrases—doing so now and then makes them seem likeable and human—but they try to minimize their use so as not to be distracting and annoying. People calling in, by contrast, might begin with praise for the host or the show, the always lurking "longtime listener, first-time caller." With such openings, callers are just being polite and expressing a flattering opinion. While hosts certainly like to hear they're doing good work and that their shows are valued, if every caller begins by voicing such praise a lot of air-time is taken away from the subject under discussion. Hosts, then, often turn to the curt, "What's your question?" Out comes a string of fillers and missteps as callers try to ask the questions they had in mind. It's not necessarily that callers are less thoughtful or less intelligent than broadcasters; it's just that they're less practiced in professional speech. And there's certainly a degree of nervousness in knowing your voice is being broadcast to the world. Listening to such a variety of voices over an hour can quickly acclimate you toward hearing the sounds and cadence that distinguish people of different ages, different cultures, different occupations.

Exercise: Listen, Now

There's a reason that so many of Hemingway's most memorable scenes are set in bars and cafés. They provide an immediate setting to hear all varieties of conversations. Find places where people have conversations in public: restaurants, sidewalks, shopping malls, coffee shops, hotel lobbies, airports, bus stops, barber shops, and beauty salons. Spend at least an hour in three such places, listening in for how people speak to one another. Look especially for the types of conversations that might belong to a Hemingway story—for instance, couples who argue over seemingly insignificant concerns (drinks, what movie to see, what meal to order) that reveal more about their relationship than what's on the surface.

Location	Conversation Overheard	People Involved	Tensions Created
Chicago's Venice café	Arguments over the menu	Low-life gangster and diner habitués	Restaurant policy vs. customer desire

What's the Point? The purpose of this exercise is twofold. 1. Continue developing your "writer's ear" by listening to the qualities of actual speech. 2. Begin capturing such dialogue moments that might spark enough character tension for the fire of a complete story. And if you're caught eavesdropping, you can always explain that you're doing the work of a good writer: research.

What They Say Is Who They Are:
Dialogue and Characterization

After you've begun the fieldwork of listening to people's speech as a writer, the challenge becomes translating those observations into effective characterization and plot use. And just because you, the writer, have become a good listener, doesn't mean that your characters now are. The man in "Hills Like White Elephants" is so intent upon convincing Jig to have an abortion—convincing her that she wants to have an abortion—that he misses everything she says about how their relationship will change. Jig asks, "Can't we maybe stop talking?"[85] But he goes on, trying to make her "realize" what she wants. Readers, however, realize that here is a character bent on not hearing what's said to him and using the power of his relationship with Jig to cajole her into complying with his desires.

Writers on Papa Nadine Gordimer, the 1991 recipient of the Nobel Prize for Literature, credited Papa with being able to listen for what her own characters left unspoken.

What your characters say and how they say it is realistic when it comes from a fully developed sense of who they are. Thinking through a character's backstory and profile is an essential step in crafting dialogue that readers will believe (see Chapter 3). When your character enters a restaurant, is he someone who asks, "Could I see the menu, please?" Or does he say, "I'll have a look at the menu." If he's a Hemingway character, it might be: "What's good?"

The rhythms and accents of speech in "The Killers" can best be seen in the difference between Al and Max's city-speak and the talk of the townspeople. In what ways does the speech of the two killers set them apart from the small-town Midwesterners?

The first clue that Al and Max are, in fact, gangsters comes from their dialogue. After they're told a second time that they can't have anything off the dinner menu, Max says, "Everything we want's the dinner, eh? That's the way you work it."[86] Max sees George's refusal to give him anything from the dinner menu before 6 P.M. as a scam, as George's way of "working" the diner's racket. Why does he see the dinner menu as a racket? Because he's a gangster.

"The Killers" could have opened by telling us Al and Max come from Chicago. It could have begun with the detail about Al and Max's derby hats or black overcoats. Doing so, however, would make it something other than a Hemingway story. By leading with the story's dialogue, Papa consciously introduces both character and conflict through the way Max talks to George.

The most repeated line in "The Killers" is Al and Max's calling George and Nick "bright boys." Al and Max are, of course, men of action—the button men sent to kill Andreson. Their sarcasm shows the disdain they have for "thinkers." They dislike people who think they know how the world operates, like George who believes "it's all right." But Al and Max also have a plan, one that gives them a sense of power over George and Nick. Before telling him of their plan to "kill a Swede," Max taunts George: "What do you think's going to happen?"[87]

As Al and Max give up on Andreson coming to the diner, Al complains that Max talks too much, unnecessarily giving up their plans. Max replies, "Oh, what the hell . . . We got to keep amused, haven't we?"[88] But Al and Max's gangster twang isn't just for their amusement—it's also for our amusement as readers. And for establishing them as characters. And for setting up the tensions of the story.

What about the speech of those characters living in Summit? How do the voices of this suburban town contrast with the talk of Chicago?

In the first dialogue of the story, Hemingway starts us on George's characterization—there's no "howdy," "hello," or "good afternoon." George is pragmatic and to-the-point with his "What's yours?"[89] when he asks Al and Max what they'd like to eat. It's as pragmatic as the advice he gives Nick on understanding the violence and despair at the story's end: it's most practical to put it out of your mind, to get on with your life.

With Nick, it's significant that "The Killers" is the only story of his adolescence that's not set in Michigan. His dialogue in this story shows a character coming of age, a character between the woods of his Michigan youth and the war of his frontline manhood. The most repeated subject of his sentences in "The Killers" is the first-person "I," a sign that he hasn't grown beyond himself yet.

For Ole Andreson, his despair has led him to give up on doing anything about the threat to his life. He's a character entirely accepting of his environment—fatal as it is—and that's reflected in his dialogue where he mirrors the words Nick says to him. Nick says, "George thought I better come and tell you *about it*." But Ole says, "There isn't anything I can do *about it*." Nick: "I'll tell you *what they were like*." Ole: "I don't want to know *what they were like*."[90] Stylistically, of course, Hemingway had learned to use such repetition while under the tutelage of Gertrude Stein. But here the effect of Ole repeating Nick's words tells us something unique about his character, his inability to respond to Nick with any force. The repetition signals Ole's submission to the forces out to kill him.

Even Mrs. Bell's exchange with Nick as he's leaving tells us something about the people of Summit. Nick presumes that she's the owner of "Hirsch's rooming-house,"[91] but Mrs. Bell corrects him. She explains that Mrs. Hirsh owns the boarding house, and she's only the superintendent. Why does Papa include this disconnected bit of dialogue between Nick and a supporting cast? For one reason, it suggests a depth of realism to the story, adding a layer to the town through a quick comment from a character. But it also suggests something about those who live in this suburb of Chicago. Like George manning the counter at "Henry's lunch-room,"[92] no one seems to own a stake in Summit itself.

While the two broad categories of characters in "The Killers" distinguishes Al and Max from the rest of the town, the dialogue of the locals further differentiates the man behind the diner counter from the visiting adolescent, the retired boxer on the lam from his boardinghouse caretaker. Remember, too, that what characters say about each other can rarely be taken at face value—and characters' perceptions of themselves will often conflict with what other characters or narrators say about them. Mrs. Bell explains that Andreson is "an awfully nice man" who is "just as gentle."[93] But what Mrs. Bell hears as nice and gentle in the Swede's speech might just as easily be seen as that of a fighter-turned-defeatist, stoically accepting his fate.

Exercise: You Are What You Say

For the list of character types below, describe how you imagine their speech would set them apart from other characters. Then, draft one line of dialogue that captures the essence of that speech.

Character Types	Description of Their Speech	Drafted Dialogue
Max, a prohibition-era gangster	Threatening and presumptive	"That's the way you work it."
A small-town local		
A city dweller		
A salesperson		
A doctor		
A big-game hunter		
A NASCAR driver		
A waitress		
A socialite		
A teenage football player		

What's the Point? The purpose of this exercise is to begin linking the qualities of a line of dialogue to a unique understanding of the character speaking. Hemingway himself was a man of action, and he saw his characters defined through what they did. The boxer, the matador, the hit man, or the war hero all become who they are through their actions. It's necessary, then, to see characters' speech as an important extension of who they are.

Dialogue and the Game of Tag

A dialogue tag is used to identify the character speaking a specific line, as in: "Jane said," 'You're going to clean up that mess, aren't you?'" Readers know immediately which character is speaking.

A common mistake of novice writers, however, is to oversell a line of dialogue through the use of the artful tag. *"Jane said"* becomes: *"Jane snarled."* Or, *"Jake said"* becomes *"Jake retorted*, 'I'll clean it up when I get time.'" When writers try to show off an astounding vocabulary, their manuscripts become littered with the flare-ups of an overly active thesaurus. Sound writing is replaced by a search for variations on "said": begged or bellowed, cried or complained, demurred or demanded, enunciated or exclaimed, pronounced or proclaimed.

Such ornamental flourishes distract readers from what characters are saying—and the point of dialogue is precisely to focus readers on what's being said. They appear amateurish. Writers who use dialogue tags in this way try to give them the secondary purpose of telling readers how to interpret the dialogue, rather than allowing the dialogue to stand on its own. Like the difference between showing and telling in descriptive writing, artful dialogue tags force readers to dwell on the frame rather than the painting itself. While it's okay to use such dialogue tags sparingly—very sparingly—the silent and direct "said" or "asked" typically accomplish all that's needed.

Hemingway's advice for knowing what dialogue tags to use? Keep it simple, keep it direct. Simple and direct. And as often as possible, do away with them altogether.

Let's look at the beginning of "The Killers" for how Papa establishes his characters and sets us amid their conversation. Remember that while we're being introduced to these characters as readers, the pair of outsiders and the pair of townspeople are being introduced to each other as well:

The door of Henry's lunch-room opened and two men came in. They sat down at the counter.

"What's yours?" George asked *them.*

"I don't know," one of the men said. *"What do you want to eat, Al?"*

"I don't know, said *Al. "I don't know what I want to eat."*[94]

Asked, said, and said. Hemingway keeps it straightforward. With over 200 lines of dialogue in "The Killers," Papa uses tags other than "asked" or "said" only four times. Whenever Papa steers away from the simple and direct in his dialogue tags, it's toward good purpose and not the arbitrary use of a florid style. He uses "explained" early on to illustrate the awkwardness in George's argument with Al and Max over what time dinner's available. He uses "called" twice to emphasize a conversation carried on between the lunch counter and the kitchen. And he uses "went on" as Nick recounts being held hostage to Andreson—emphasizing Nick's continuing to tell the story even though it seems ridiculous.

With his choice of dialogue tags identifying who's speaking in this initial exchange, Hemingway sets readers amid the points of view of those in the diner. When Max first speaks, he's described as "one of the men." And it's only because he calls Al by name that his dialogue tag reads "said Al." The mystery of finding out the name of the "first man," the man arguing with George, sustains readers through the story's first pages. By contrast, George is identified straightway, quickly giving readers the name of the man behind the counter. (In a like manner, Nick Adams is identified by his complete name in the fifth paragraph, although he doesn't speak for some time.)

One of Hemingway's great innovations in dialogue use came from the realization that once characters are established in a conversation with each other (even if in a brief "first man" or "second man"), it's possible to do away altogether with the dialogue tags separating them. Passages of dialogue in "The Killers" go on for several paragraphs without any tag identifying who is speaking. Readers can breeze through these passages, picking up directions on which character is speaking from the characteristics of voice and the natural rhythm of Character A talking, then Character B talking. While other writers had used this free exchange of dialogue, Hemingway did it to such an extent that the technique and rhythms of this style of writing became uniquely his.

Dialogue Balanced with a Descriptive Tag

What if you want to indicate something about the tone of a character's speech, but want to avoid those overly artful dialogue tags? Another device for indicating how a line of dialogue might be read is to couple it with a concise description of what the character's doing while speaking. A benefit of using brief description this way is that it accomplishes what the artful dialog tag intended—clarifying how a spoken line should be understood, suggesting an inference not immediately apparent—but with none of the awkwardness. This technique is classic Hemingway, short and true.

Notice in the following examples how Hemingway hinges a line of dialogue with a description of about the same length, establishing a balanced rhythm. The dialogue and the description work to complete each other. (Descriptions are indicated in italics.) Explaining the killers' reaction as George watches them eat, Hemingway writes: "'What are you looking at?' *Max looked at George.*" Directing George's movements from the kitchen, Al says, "'Stand a little further along the bar. You move a little to the left, Max.' *He was like a photographer arranging for a group picture.*" When Nick is freed after the killers leave, Hemingway writes: "'Say,' he said. 'What the hell?' *He was trying to swagger it off.*"[95]

Exercise: Experimenting with What Your Characters Say

Select two or three of the characters from the profiles you created in Chapter 3. Then, write a scene (of two to three pages) where you establish their characters almost entirely through what they say and how they say it. You might try rewriting one of our Chapter 3 exercises that were geared toward character development and see how a shift to emphasizing dialogue changes the scene's characterization. If 80 to 90 percent of your scene relys upon dialogue rather than narration or description, you'll be close to the ratio found in stories such as "The Killers" or "Hills Like White Elephants." Now, experiment by removing as many dialogue tags as you can while still keeping it apparent which character is speaking. You might establish the rhythm of the scene (and your writing) by balancing elements of dialogue with descriptive tags.

What's the Point? Dialogue was Hemingway's principle way of creating believable characters from what might otherwise have been caricatures. Relying upon dialogue in this way is also a useful means of speeding up the pace of a scene, balancing it against the moments of description or narration where Hemingway's staccato sentences slow down and detail the moment.

A lesser writer might have tried forcing the described tone through inappropriate artful tags: "'What are you looking at?' Max challenged." "Al ordered, 'Stand a little further along the bar.'" Or, "'Say,' Nick complained, 'What the hell?'" These use the style of the wrench when something subtler is needed.

Dialogue off the Beat

One last word on a dialogue technique that's specific to Hemingway's style: an exchange between characters that shifts order without warning.

In a typical exchange of dialogue, readers expect different lines of speech to switch between characters, using paragraph breaks to set up a "he said," then "she said," then "he said" pattern. This is especially true when dialogue tags have been entirely removed.

But in stories like "A Clean Well-Lighted Place" or novels such as *The Sun Also Rises*, Papa played with the usual beat of his characters' conversation through a technique literary critics have come to call "anti-metronomic" dialogue. An exchange between two characters typically moves back and forth on a regular rhythm, the way that the pendulum of a metronome clicks back and forth with each oscillation. In a typical story, when no dialogue tags are used, this switch between speakers is suggested only by a paragraph break and an indentation.

Hemingway occasionally separated two lines of dialogue, however, which came from the same character (rather than switching between speakers). In "A Clean, Well-Lighted Place," the best known instance, the older waiter says both of these unattributed lines in sequence:

"He must be eighty years old."
"Anyway I should say he was eighty."[96]

Literary critics at first debated whether or not this use of anti-metronomic dialogue was an oversight on Papa's part. The many revisions to the story and Hemingway's use of the technique in other works, however, show that he did use it intentionally. It shouldn't be surprising that a writer who changed how we read dialogue in a story experimented with ways of changing the rhythm of a character's speech. And those initiated into this special style of Hemingway's dialogue know to look for the paragraphed pause of one character's voice.

Mimicking Hemingway: Dialogue in a Diner

Keeping in mind the lessons of Hemingway's dialogue we've discussed in this chapter, you might try your hand at rewriting "The Killers" set in a twenty-first-century restaurant. Since the greasy-spoon diners of Hemingway's 1920s are less of a fixture today, you might imagine how Al and Max's mission would play out in the customer-satisfaction establishments of American cities and towns. In place of "Henry's Lunch-Room" might be the family-friendly chain store, "Applebutter's." Gone is George's curt and to-the-point "What's yours?" replaced by an ever-smiling, "Welcome to Applebutter's. How may I help you?" Rewrite the rapport between hit men and service industry with the cadences of today's speech. And if you keep Al and Max as gruff as their Capone-like archetypes, you might end up with a fine satire.

Dialogue over Disaster

Dialogue in "The Short Happy Life of Francis Macomber" plays a primary role in the way three central characters exert their power over each other: Robert Wilson, a hunter, sleeps with Margot, the wife of Macomber, the man he's leading on safari. After Macomber's death, Wilson barrages Margot with a list of what needed to be done to convince the authorities that she's not responsible. Margot only responds by repeating "Stop it" a total of six times. Finally, she says, "Oh, please stop it." And Wilson says, ending the story, "That's better. Please is much better. Now I'll stop."[97] Write a scene of dialogue that mimics this moment between two characters who have just experienced some tragedy or disaster. One of the characters—perhaps the woman over the man this time—uses the exchange to punish the other. Why does the character want the other to submit by saying "please"?

What We Talk about When We Argue

"Hills Like White Elephants" provides a memorable dialogue of Hemingway's characters arguing over how they talk with one another— a sign that the man and woman have something serious to discuss (an abortion), but they begin by fighting over how to talk to one another. Take a moment and read through the story; the dialogue should go quickly. Slow down, though, and notice when the couple begins talking about their drinks, Jig compares hers to licorice. One brief remark is seemingly about their drinks: "all the things you've waited so long for." With its undertones of pregnancy and family, however, what's implied is the root of the couple's conversation. They quickly turn to arguing over the way they dance around the subject: "Oh, cut it out." "You started it."[98] Imagine two characters romantically involved who have something different to fight about—a cheating spouse, a fatal illness, a failed mortgage—and rewrite Hemingway's exchange with a different "surface" subject. Instead of sparring over the taste of a drink, perhaps they're arguing over what movie to watch, what restaurant to eat at, or what present to buy their child. You might examine the 2006 film *Babel*, written by Guillermo Arriaga, for echoes of such Papa dialogue in Brad Pitt and Cate Blanchette's argument about ice for their drinks in the wake of an infant son's death.

The Green Hills of *Hemingway:*
Setting and Description

5

"Your first seeing of a country is a very

valuable one."

(*Green Hills of Africa*[99])

Any casual tour of Hemingway's titles reveals the significance of place to him: "The Snows of Kilimanjaro," "Up in Michigan," "A Clean, Well-Lighted Place," *Across the River and into the Trees*, *The Old Man and the Sea*. The list goes on.

The "setting" of a story includes, most simply, the where and when that its events take place. In terms of artistic technique, setting is brought about by a writer's ability to describe, to picture the physical landscape or appearance of characters. But Hemingway claimed that writers—good writers, anyhow—did not "describe" in any pure sense. This might seem odd, since setting and description are so very linked to each other. Doesn't description provide the details for readers to form a mental image of a fictional world?

Papa's prohibition against description, whether he knew it from experience or reading, goes back to the historical meaning of "describe." In the word's initial sense, describe meant literally to "copy off" or to "sketch in writing or drawing." De-scribing was a type of "putting down" of reality into words, the same work that a photograph or film might do. Hemingway saw description as a lesser form of writing partly due to the frequent assumptions that his work was entirely autobiographical—that a work such as "The Short Happy Life of Francis Macomber" was more memoir than imagination. Whenever he talked about the craft of writing, Hemingway emphasized his powers of invention that he needed as an artist in creating world-class prose. It isn't enough to copy reality through a catalog of minutiae, describing each veined leaf, each forked branch, each knotted trunk, to write a forest into life. Writers don't copy from detail. They create from knowledge.

You might think of Hemingway's descriptive technique, then, in the sense of "setting" as a verb. Writers don't "describe" so much as they "set down" the essential details needed to bring a scene into imaginative life. *Describing* merely copies what is seen. *Setting* selects details that are essential and places only them on the page. *Describing* is pro forma, blindly including everything witnessed in the hope that completeness creates an emotion. *Setting* is intentional and careful, choosing the details that will lead to deliberate response.

With that sense of how Hemingway thought of description, we'll examine what role setting plays in a story, from different geographies to how changes in place can alter a reader's view of character. We'll see how Hemingway used his selective, descriptive technique in bringing landscapes and cityscapes into fictional being. And we'll see how powers of description are able to bring characters into life as part of their surroundings.

Setting the Scene: What Papa Learned from Cézanne

In talking about where he learned his ability to capture setting, Hemingway credited painters more often than he did other writers.

Many of the painters that he mentioned as influences seem complete opposites to Papa's reputation for staunch realism. Hieronymus Bosch, for instance, used symbolism extensively to represent abstract notions about sin or salvation in works such as *Ship of Fools* (c. 1490–1500), a painting showing the hedonistic folly of people drinking, gambling, and flirting. (Hemingway wrote about such habits, of course, but not from an allegorical viewpoint.) Another Netherlander influence he cited, Vincent van Gogh, had developed just as recognizable a style in painting as Hemingway would in writing. With his heavy use of bright color and distinctive brush strokes, however, Van Gogh's post-impressionistic style also appears distant from that of the spartan writer of *The Sun Also Rises*.

In common with his writing, the painters Hemingway admired had a willingness to experiment with artistic technique as a way of expressing emotional effect. Both painter and writer select color and texture, perspective and detail, to create a scene. An understanding of Hemingway's debt to them reveals, reputation aside, how Hemingway's descriptive technique blends elements of abstraction and realism alike. A story that moves its plot with only dialogue, that establishes its characters with only a touch of description, presents a carefully pared-down version of reality: A setting stripped down to its naked, evocative essentials.

Paul Cézanne was the artist that Hemingway most often credited with influencing him. Papa's contemporaries Picasso and Matisse, who had first met through Gertrude Stein, both recognized Cézanne as the "father of us all." During his Paris years, Hemingway remembered going almost every day to the Musée du Luxembourg to see the Cézannes on display there, paintings such as *L'Estaque* and *The Poplars*." On days when the light had faded in the museum, Hemingway could make his way to 27 Rue de Fleurus to see the works by Cézanne and other early modernist masters that hung in Stein and Toklas's atelier.

Hemingway was always elusive in explaining precisely how Cézanne's work influenced his descriptive writing. In *A Moveable Feast*, he wrote, "I was learning something from the painting of Cézanne that made writing simple true sentences far from enough to make the stories have the dimensions that I was trying to put in them." Cryptically, he declared the lessons a "secret."[100] Some clues into this secret come from a coda that Hemingway wrote but did not include with "Big Two-Hearted River." There, Nick Adams reveals that he "wanted to write like

Cezanne painted." As Nick conceived it, Cézanne started with the "tricks" of artistic technique, but then "broke the whole thing down and built the real thing." In order to "write about country so that it would be there like Cezanne had done it in painting," Nick understands that "you had to do it from inside yourself."[101]

That last phrase, "from inside yourself," proves key to understanding what Hemingway meant by the writer's role in creating setting rather than just copying description. Painters such as Cézanne and Van Gogh, Picasso and Matisse were not aiming for the realism of a photograph in their works. Cameras could perform such work. The canvas, the paint, the stroke of the brush: tools that conveyed the artist's imagination, not just the experience of seeing the Bay of Marseilles or the trees of Provence. The paper, the ink, the strike of the typebar: each brought Hemingway's artistic visions of Michigan woods or Pamplonan streets into fictional being.

Learning to create an effective setting in your writing, then, begins with careful observation, but it also requires an understanding of how sights, sounds, and senses create an impression of wonderment or pain. Leave the lifeless setting—the one tapped of human passion—to the scientists.

Exercise: A Country Like Cézanne

To see what so impressed Hemingway about Cézanne, track down a number of his paintings, both the oils and the watercolors. Most art museums in major cities will have a few Cézannes, and Paris's Musée d'Orsay and the Louvre have special collections. It's worth the experience of standing in front of an original—shading, size, and brush stroke are unmitigated before you. There are thousands of images to be seen on the Internet, of course, although a pixilated Cézanne isn't the same as an original painting. What emotions do the paintings suggest? Your job as a writer is to be able to pinpoint what details, what colors, what forms bring out those emotions. Now, select one painting, perhaps the view of the Mediterranean coast at L'Estaque, and describe it as a setting over two or three pages. Work on getting the emotion right through the details.

What's the Point? Hemingway credited modernist painters with teaching him how artists see the world. To be significant, setting should evoke emotion, not just duplicate reality. After you've done it with one painting, repeat the exercise with another work or artist. Does the emotion of the setting change?

What Is Setting?

In its most basic sense, "setting" refers to the backdrop in front of which a story unfolds. The "set" of a play reinforces this notion, and includes all of the furniture and properties, the lighting and scrim against which actors performs. Sets in the modern theater, however, can be quite intricate. Lights and music change the tone of a scene, walls or scaffolding assume intricate designs, and actors ascend from trapdoors or descend from above. In one production of *Macbeth*, the stage walls literally inched inward during a scene, squeezing the actor in while he gave the "Tomorrow, and tomorrow, and tomorrow" speech. Such dynamic settings interact with their performers as much as the performers interact with them.

It's in this dynamic sense of setting that you need to think of yourself as a writer shaping a changing environment as part of your story.

Hemingway's settings often brought home rarefied or distant locales to his American readers. Twentieth-century war with the fresh horrors known only to shell-shocked veterans. The Left Bank with its circles of artists. The Spanish mountains full of Republican idealists. African plains and their community of professional hunters. Caribbean waters with the secret economies of commercial fishermen. Even Papa's American settings took readers down the trails of the Midwestern backcountry or the alleys of Midwestern cities.

If Papa's fiction brought the experience of these far-away places to his readers, it also brought Papa's readers out into the world. The fan industry that sprung up around many of Hemingway's books regularly chases after the life of his characters, transforming their habits and haunts into travel vacations.

Today, you can choose from whole lines of Hemingway apparel, from Hemingway safari hats to Hemingway polo shirts. Travel agencies ship tourists on Hemingway-themed adventures to Hemingway-penned destinations, from Kansas City to Kiliman-jaro. Cuba hosts a Hemingway international fishing tournament each year. Key West has its Hemingway Days each July.

Habits of Hemingway Papa wrote several of his Michigan stories while he lived in Paris. To help him envision the setting, he kept a map of the northern part of the state on his wall.

Such interest in the places that Hemingway lived in and wrote about is a testament to his ability to capture setting in his stories as an essential part of character and action.

But setting is more than a dot on a map: it's more than the Pamplona of *The Sun Also Rises*, the Sierra de Guadarrama of *For Whom the Bell Tolls*, or the Michigan wilderness of the Nick Adams stories. An effectively used setting suggests something of location, but it also showcases landscape as part of the unfolding story. Setting includes geography, but it also includes the daily habits of characters, the atmosphere and time in which they live, the way that place influences the character of the times.

The Senses of a Setting

Good descriptive writing appeals to the senses. Whether you're describing a person or a place, the details that make your writing more than ink on a page must summon up the sensual memories of a reader. Just as well-written dialogue carries the sound of a character's voice to the reader's internal ear, the details you select in a description should play upon the senses. The human mind accesses the world through sight, sound, smell, touch, and taste. A reader's imagination enters your fiction through those same senses.

Effective characterization requires you to watch and listen to people with understanding. Effective description requires the same skills of observation. In "Monologue to the Maestro," Papa tells the aspiring writer to keep track of all the action that takes place on their fishing boat. The importance of a scene comes from the particular sights, sounds, or other senses that generate a particular emotion. If the writer gets a thrill over landing a fish, he must remember the sight of the line in the water, the clack of reel straining against the pull, the cold splash of the fish throwing water in a jump. It's getting these details straight for the reader, details linked to the senses, that can create the same emotion that the writer experiences. Telling a reader that a character is "thrilled" by catching a fish is one thing. Showing the line tightening, the reel wincing, and the character bent forward, neck stretched to get a better view of the water, is quite another.

Senses in "Big Two-Hearted River"

As an example of fine descriptive writing, there may be none better in the American tradition than Hemingway's "Big Two-Hearted River." A Nick Adams story in two parts, "Big Two-Hearted River" opens in what used to be the town of Seney. Erased in the flames of a forest fire, the town's only reminders of civilization are the railroad tracks and the foundation of chipped stone from a lost hotel. Up the hillside are the ghosts of burnt trees. The river remains, stocked with trout. And its up this river that the story follows Nick as he attempts to remind himself of the joy he found fishing these waters with friends in a time before war.

The most important sense that Papa relies upon in opening "Big Two-Hearted River" is sight. The vision of the Michigan wilderness—charred and burned at first, but then alive and wild—revives Nick in his return to woods and river and adolescent innocence. Over the space of just three early paragraphs, Hemingway uses the verbs "looked," "watched," or "saw" twelve times. Most of these looking verbs have to do with Nick's surveying of the land and river, but even the trout are "looking" to keep near the bed of a deep river pool.

As Nick moves deeper into the wilderness, Hemingway's description begins to incorporate the other senses. It's clear that the sensual experience of the river and the woods is important to both Hemingway and his character alike. Where Nick pauses to sit on a log, Hemingway writes that he "did not want to rush his sensations any." Stepping out of the river while fishing for trout, he feels the water run down his legs, wiggling his feet in his "squelchy" shoes. Here Papa suggests the feel of the water, but in the word "squelchy" also the suctioned sound of Nick pulling his foot against a waterlogged sole.[102]

This use of sensation—of sight, of touch, of sound—is especially important in understanding Papa's technique of fashioning description after Cézanne. Nick imagines just how Cézanne would paint this view of the Big Two-Hearted River. But Nick doesn't limit the painter to sight. To understand the landscape as Cézanne would, Nick the writer descends into the river. In a striking sentence, Hemingway writes: "The water was cold and actual." *Cold* and *actual*. The coldness of the water is realized in the act of feeling it. And it's in capturing that sensation for the page that allows a setting to live as art. For Nick, for Hemingway, for Cézanne, it's in that sensation that the artist matters.

Exercise: Sound and Sensation

Locate yourself in a place meaningful to a character—a bend of river for fishing, a favorite café, or even within a cold-water apartment. Take careful note of the sounds in that place: its ticks and twitters, its clacks and cackles. List as many layers of sound as you can, what's taking place both near and far, what's loud and soft. Don't rush the feelings. Now, write two to three pages describing how your character reacts to those sounds. You're on track to Hemingway's style if you can suggest your character's inner emotions by describing only his or her outward actions, not overly telling readers that the character feels nostalgic, frightened, or saddened.

What's the Point? This exercise gets you to focus on creating the sensory details that bring a setting into being. Repeat as necessary for sight, smell, touch, and taste.

Effective Setting Takes Action

The most relevant uses of setting in both fiction and nonfiction writing blend both the action and background as integral parts of a scene. This means thinking of your setting as an active and living element of your story. In this way setting can be as significant a character within a story as those modeled on people. Certainly, the title of *The Old Man and the Sea* suggests a potent relationship between one character and another, protagonist and antagonist, that would be skewed if the story were *The Old Man and the Marlin*.

Setting is not a still life. Many beginning writers (and some who are published) mistake setting as something stationary. Rather than using setting as a moving part of a scene's drama, they pause to detail the curtains. Should readers choose to linger over such passages, they must wade through a catalog of static details irrelevant to a scene as it comes into focus. As the hero glances out a window to glimpse his love passing by, the narrative stops for us to learn the fabric of the drapes, the frayed knots of its stitching, the metal of the rod, the wood of its frame, the splintering crack of its glass. Overloading a scene with static description can pull away from the narrative.

It may be useful to think of setting as part of a movie rather than a photograph. That is, successful settings become part of a scene's action. Rather than describing the world your characters inhabit as a moment frozen in time, envision it as a video camera might. Move through the set in three-dimensional space, describing how people interact with it or how parts of the environment interact with each other. If it's a wilderness scene, what is the wind doing to the grass? What is the lion doing lurking behind its blades? If a cityscape, how is the crowd pressing down the sidewalk? If we follow them, where does the crowd lead?

The Life of the Setting

Consider the way setting takes on an active life with its characters in Hemingway's "Landscape with Figures," a short story set during the Spanish Civil War. While this story went unpublished while Hemingway was alive, Papa suggested it in 1939 for an unrealized collection that included the idea of what would become *The Old Man and the Sea*. Following Hemingway's classic protagonist and antagonist characterization, Edwin Henry, a code figure wise to the habits of warfare, leads a camera crew that is set to film a pending battle from a bombed-out apartment house. A cocky Brit, referred to only as the "Great Authority," joins them on the front line, bringing along a female American reporter. Hapless in front of the enemy, the Authority's arrogance allows the glint off his binoculars and his absurd steel helmet to draw fire from the fascist artillery. The title "Landscape with Figures" comes from the vision of a battle taking place on an outlying hill: the dying soldiers are diminished in the distance, enough to make the scene seem like the picture of a battle rather than a reality.

Hemingway's opening paragraph describes the principle setting of the story, the apartment house that Ed's crew refers to as the "Old Homestead." Papa does not describe the scene, however, in the static fashion of telling readers what the result of direct blasts from explosive shells does to a building. Using Edwin as a narrator, Hemingway inhabits the building, showing it in motion. The busted elevator no longer works as the beam that it moves up and down on is twisted. And several marble stairs are broken so that passersby must ascend along the edges to avoid falling through. Doors open into third-floor rooms no longer there, but fourth floor rooms are not only undamaged but have working plumbing. It's through the motion that the setting comes alive: the lost movement of the elevator, the motion of people walking up a staircase, the swinging of a door out into empty space.

One difference that comes from showing readers the "Old Homestead" as if walking along on a tour of the building is that a sense of dramatic tension immediately develops. The implication is that we might fall through the broken marble stairs. The hole in the staircase suddenly has a consequence to it that it wouldn't otherwise have if readers were directly told that the stairs were damaged. It's this tension that makes Hemingway's description the difference between creative writing and an insurance adjustor's damage report.

Effective Setting Is Specific and Concrete

Imagine this scene: you and a lover sit down at a restaurant, intent on sharing a bottle of wine. The waiter walks up, wipes his wet hands on an apron, and pulls out a black notebook from a back pocket:

"Good evening, folks. Can I start you off with some drinks?"

"Sure," your lover says. "Why don't you order, dear?"

"We'd like a bottle of wine."

"Here's our drink list." The waiter flips open a menu that had been standing on the table. "We no longer have the 2006 vidal blanc, but the rest are in."

"We'll have a bottle of wine."

"Any that you like. Except the 2006 vidal, like I said."

"What kind do you have, then?"

Pointing down the list, he says, "Reds. Whites. Sparkling on the back."

"Okay, we'll have a bottle of white, then."

"Which one?"

"Oh, I don't know."

"Dear, would you just pick one?"

"Why can't we just get a bottle of wine? We used to try any new drink we wanted. Just bring us a bottle of wine, would you?"

Any more than ordering "Mexican food" in a Tex-Mex restaurant, or "Chinese food" in a Chinese restaurant, you couldn't ask for a "bottle of wine" and expect not to be met with blank stares of frustration. It's the same with descriptive writing.

Beginning writers are often told to be specific in a description. As such, they write, "The fish was in the net." Specific enough, right? We do have two very real objects, a fish and a net. So has our descriptive setting come into being? Not quite.

Precision in Expression

Abstractions are words that don't directly appeal to the senses. They're removed a step or two or three from the felt world. "Captivity" is a complex idea, and to the inmate locked down in a prison cell it can feel very real. It might be the same emotion shared by our netted fish. But you can't feel captivity in the same way you can touch the iron bars of the cell, their chipped paint flaking away the hours. These details about the bars, about the paint are what make a setting.

But "fish" is a type of abstraction too, a generalization about creatures of many types. Imagine for a moment all of the animals you could include under the word "fish." Our original sentence, "The fish was in the net," could refer to a goldfish circling an aquarium. It might refer to a brook trout, pulling against a leader in a Michigan stream. It might be a cod, crowded into a sea-trawler's catch. Or taken in a metaphorical sense, the "fish was in the net" might come from a detective's description of trapping a wanted fugitive.

The context of the story in which you'd write such a sentence would obviously shape your reader's understanding of what type of "fish" is meant. But, taken out of context, such a sentence reveals how vague language can be, even when we might think we're being specific. The problem with "the fish was in the net" on its own is that readers aren't given enough sensory details to form a clear mental image of what you intend. Even if it is a brook trout, how does this brook trout stand out from all others?

More often than not, you should narrow down word choice to the "true" word whenever possible. If you're always using broad categories, like "fish" or "bird" or "vehicle," readers never get the feeling of the uniqueness of your setting.

At other times, beginning writers will provide too much detail, as in the heavily burdened styles we discussed in Chapter 2. Readers don't need a photographic catalog of your setting's minute nuances. They need enough to get the emotional effect that you're going for. In "Big Two-Hearted River," for instance, Hemingway doesn't specify the species of trout Nick is after, but the story isn't a naturalist handbook.

Papa Says This lesson of emphasizing the concrete had a political lesson for Hemingway too. In *A Farewell to Arms*, Frederic Henry learns the difference between the romance of war and its reality: "Abstract words such as glory, honor, courage or hallow were obscene beside the concrete names of roads, the names of rivers, the numbers of villages, the numbers of regiments."[103] Hemingway's portrait of the disabused soldier places him in the similar tradition of Stephen Crane before him or Kurt Vonnegut afterward.

Inventing Setting and the Wilderness Landscape

When Hemingway first began publishing the stories he was working on in Paris, he wrote to his father to say that he had put together several stories that were set in Michigan, the site of the family's summer vacations. He explained that "the country is always true—what happens in the stories is fiction."[104]

But the truth that Hemingway claimed for his country landscapes wasn't the truth of fact. In the same letter to his father, he explained that the waters that provided the basis for "Big Two-Hearted River" was actually the Fox River, flowing south past the town of Seney and eventually into Lake Michigan. The actual Two-Hearted River lies farther north on Michigan's Upper Peninsula and empties its waters into Lake Superior.

Why change the name of the river? Any sense of poetry tells us that Two-Hearted is a richer name than Fox. Literary critics have mined that richness for what it suggests about Nick as a character, about the person he was before the war, and the person who returns afterward. Or for what it suggests about the two sides of the river itself, the waters that Nick fishes in and the tangled marsh that he refuses to enter. Hemingway, often emphasizing the literal, let the significance of the name carry with it whatever associations readers found.

Taking License

The river's name wasn't the only difference between the landscape outside the historical Seney and the one that found its way into Papa's fiction. The fictional Seney in which Nick Adams alights from the train has been freshly destroyed by fire. The historical fire that completely devastated Seney, Michigan, occurred in 1891, eight years before Hemingway was born. In the story's first sentence, Nick watches the train disappear as its tracks bend around a hill. The train tracks that run through the real Seney, however, run straight east-to-west for as far as the eyes can see. And as he sets off on his fishing trip he abandons the road to ascend a fictional hill scorched by the fire. The real Seney sits on a flat plain.

The truth that Hemingway meant for the way in which he presented landscape, then, came from the emotional effect that he intended to create from his settings. Setting functions in "Big Two-Hearted River" as a type of mirror for what Nick is feeling, and it is Nick's impression of the fictional hills, the fictional fire-ravaged land that the story conveys. In the way that Cézanne's paintings didn't provide a photographic transcription of the Mediterranean coastline, neither does Hemingway's setting provide a factual duplication of Seney.

Exercise: The Composite Setting

In fashioning the setting for "Big Two-Hearted River," Hemingway took some realistic elements of the environment around Seney, Michigan, but he culled details from other places to give the story the effect he wanted. Select three different places that you're familiar with—perhaps three different restaurants, three different rivers, or three different sporting arenas. List the descriptive qualities that make each location distinct. Then, write a two to three page description from this list that blends the qualities of each. Keep in mind the lessons of selecting your details for the effect you intend to have on readers, and fill the setting with characters and their actions.

What's the Point? Hemingway chose details from his experience and invented other details to create settings that presented only what was essential to an emotional truth, the feeling created from an imagined setting. In picking out details from multiple locations, you'll be less prone to keeping a close fidelity to any one.

Papa Says When drafting the "Big Two-Hearted River," Hemingway boasted that there wasn't much of a plot, even though the story was quite long. He explained instead that the story's best quality was its depiction of the country. The setting of the story, and Nick's relationship to that country, seemed significant enough to replace the need for an overly active plot.[105]

Setting and the City

Hemingway's reputation may rest primarily at the edges of civilization, in the wilderness of Michigan's North Country, in the waters around the Florida Keys, or in the grasslands of African savannahs.

But the town and the city also played an important role in his fiction: the Paris and Pamplona of *The Sun Also Rises*, the Madrid of "The Capital of the World," or the suburban Summit of "The Killers." The city and all of its dangers could provide just as much insight into the test of a character as any other wilderness.

The tempo and the sounds of the city are often characteristically thought to be at odds with the country. But the skills you use as a writer in inventing each type of setting are the same.

Let's look at how Papa evoked the tempo and the traffic, the clatter and the crowds of Paris in *The Sun Also Rises*. Jake Barnes is sitting outside a café, watching the city settle into the evening as the street prostitutes (*poules*) go by. Notice the layers of sense (touch, sight, sound) that Hemingway excites in just one sentence.

> *It was a warm spring night and I sat at a table on the terrace of the Napolitain after Robert had gone, watching it get dark and the electric signs come on, and the red and green stop-and-go traffic signal, and the crowd going by, and the horse-cabs clippety-clopping along the edge of the solid taxi traffic, and the poules going by, singly and in pairs, looking for the evening meal.*[106]

Here, our writer of the lean sentence abandons his trademark style to build a city scene that swells to life. We begin with the pedestrian-enough detail of a "warm spring night," perched as Jake is to witness the unfolding moment. From there, the rhythm of the sentence conveys the pace of the city traffic. The signs light up against the dark. The phrasing of "red-and-green" balances against "stop-and-go" to suggest the start-stop tempo of the street. The "clippety-clopping" echoes the sound of hooves against street stones. The prostitutes fit naturally into this environment and its rhythms, moving "singly-and-in-pairs."

The scene recalls an earlier story, "My Old Man," where a boy and his father sit outside the Café de la Paix. Watching the "streams of people" and "all sorts of guys," the boy narrator describes a similar city scene but through the lens of youth:

> *Gee, I remember the funny people that used to go by. Girls around supper time looking for somebody to take them out to eat and they'd speak to my old man and he'd make some joke at them in French and they'd pat me on the head and go on.*[107]

The prostitutes trolling for supper and the busyness of the Parisian street have a rather different tone, specifically in the boy's sense of the streetwalking "girls" versus Jake's awareness of them as prostitutes. Jake's description also makes the *poules* equal in a series of mechanical street devices—cabs and taxies, signs and signals. The boy notes the girls' kindness toward him and his father.

While both city scenes have auras to fit their narrators, the backdrop of the street traffic provides a similar canvas against which important supporting characters are introduced. As Jake's first futile interest in a woman, Georgette emerges from the passing crowd after he makes eye contact with her. Georgette's passing by, pausing only for a few hours of drinks and dancing in the plot, fits precisely with the fleeting rhythms of the street. With the boy narrating "My Old Man," the daughter of an American woman smiles back, giving him hope that she'll return some-day so he can talk to her. The promise of the girl stopping by the café again becomes a hope shared with his gambling father. The details that bring Georgette and the American girl to life are as much the setting as their looks or personality. And you couldn't imagine their characters—fleeting love interests that they are—amid any other setting.

Setting as Internal Landscape

Whether they're among the snow-crested Silvretta Alps or the darkened corridors of Spanish cafés, Hemingway's characters always hold a special relationship with their settings. Francis Macomber's being so out of place on the African safari is what awakens him before the lion—he's so removed from his familiar foreign court games that he can come alive in his short, happy life. Other characters are as much a part of their environment as any tree or building would be.

In shaping the setting of a story, you should consider how characters are essential parts of their environment. External setting can provide readers with insight into the internal land-scapes of a character's mind. After Catherine Barkley's death in childbirth, Frederic Henry walks out into the rain to return to his hotel at the end of *A Farewell to Arms*. While that clos-ing gesture may seem cold on Henry's part, it invites readers to think back on the moments when rain has played a subtle but important role in the plot. It rains with the coming of cholera. It rains when Henry comes down with jaundice. It rains when enemy artillery showers the Italian lines during the Caporetto

retreat. Rain, an element of the setting, functions as a foreshadowing device that signals coming defeat in the plot. But it also
suggests something about Henry's state of mind, the despair he
faces after the death of Cat.

Papa Says John Dos Passos had sent Hemingway a critique of
Death in the Afternoon. Papa responded in kind with a critique of 1919,
the second volume of "old Dos's" U.S.A. Trilogy: "Remember to get the
weather in your god damned book—weather is very important."[108]

Nick Adams's relationship with the Michigan wilderness
in "Big Two-Hearted River" is an exceptional example of
Hemingway using a setting to suggest the internal turmoil of
a character. Hemingway scholars agree that it's clear Nick has
just returned from World War I and suffers from the shock of
what he witnessed in that war. Hemingway himself referred to
Nick's wartime experiences this way in part of the story that
he cut out. Within "Big Two-Hearted River" itself, however,
there's no mention made of the war. It's clear that something
is deeply troubling Nick. He's returned to the river in the hope
of renewal, but the only clues readers have to that process are
found in the burned-over countryside and the recesses of the
wilderness.

It's in the Details

For this reason, the details that Hemingway altered in
describing Seney, Michigan, reveal the ways in which he saw
landscape connected with Nick's inner suffering. The burned
woods and destroyed town suggest the wartime destruction that
Nick survived—not in the hills or cities of Europe but here in
the heart of America, the internal land of his youth. When Nick

scatters a flight of grasshoppers as he walks along the road, he notices that they're all black. From living in the burned out area, soot had covered their normal colors of yellow or red. There are only two lines of speech in "Big Two-Hearted River" (Nick is the lone character), and it's significant that the first comes from Nick telling the grasshopper to fly away from the scorched earth. The second is a muttered cry to Jesus Christ in delight at eating his campfire supper. The setting of burned countryside, the destroyed town, but the living grasshopper mirrors Nick's own emotional experience. Later, the part of the river that disappears into the swamp suggests the trouble Nick has yet to confront. In this way, setting gives readers a glimpse into Nick's soul where the only part of the iceberg seen on the page suggests an objective description of the wilderness.

"Now I Lay Me," another Nick Adams story, transforms a similar river setting into a rather different emotional effect. As a lieutenant stationed in Italy during World War I, Nick avoids sleep after having been "blown up at night." To entertain himself while awake, Nick imagines fishing trout streams back home. When he ran out of bait, he would find other insects to use, especially grasshoppers that he threw into the river to watch them float along the current and then disappear as the trout took them. Again, Hemingway keeps his setting on the surface of Nick's imagination. But the implication of the grasshopper powerless in the currents of the river, not free to fly away to a new setting, suggests Nick's own fear of death amongst the currents of the war.

Exercise: Turning the Inside Out

Create a setting where you suggest the emotions of a character by the way you present the details of the scene, not by directly telling readers what a character is thinking. In two to three pages, detail a setting in such a way that brings a character's inner life out into the world. Don't pronounce what a character's feeling. And likewise don't use the types of heavy-handed modifiers of adjectives and adverbs that Hemingway deplored. You'll also want to surprise us: stay away from the clichés of sunny days and happiness, rainy Mondays and sadness. Use a sun-baked field to suggest a character's hangover. A swimming pool to suggest a character's cowardliness.

What's the Point? Like setting a description through action, connecting environment to your characters is an important way to suggest its significance. Hemingway was an "objective" writer, though, not romanticizing the landscape in the highly stylized ways of Poe or Hawthorne. To hone your technique in the way Hemingway did will require a sense of subtlety and indirect inference.

Describing People

While Nick Adams may struggle to write landscapes the way Cezanne did, he knows that he gets people right—that creating believable characters is easy. With writing so character-driven as Hemingway's, it's easy to believe this about Papa's early talents too. As Nick saw it in "On Writing," people were such a mystery that all you had to do was get their dialogue down. If readers believe what they hear coming out of a character's mouth, they'll easily buy the absurdities and nuances of personality with which you fill his head.

Yet details about a character's description outside of dialogue were important to Hemingway's writing too. In *Death in the Afternoon*, Hemingway describes the difficulty he had in describing the bullfighting technique of Domingo Hernandorena. Not a bullfighter himself, Hemingway wondered how to convey the sense of Hernandorena being nervous and unable to control his feet in front of the bull, finally dropping to both knees. What descriptive detail could capture this shameful feat? For Papa it was the "clean, clean unbearably clean whiteness of the thigh bone" while the rest of the matador's clothing was covered in dirt.[109]

Unfolding Character Description and Plot Together

Dialogue aside, then, the physical description of a person holds an important part in characterization.

In the chapter on Hemingway's techniques of character invention, we discussed the creation of character psychology and how to present characters as elements in a story (primary, secondary, supporting and so on). But while the style of shirt a character wears can tell us something about her personality—frayed denim? pressed cotton?—outward appearance fits in with other elements of setting. That is, a character's description should be active with the scene.

One way of achieving that dynamism is to introduce the specifics of a character's physical description as they become essential to elements of the plot, not necessarily all at once in the first paragraph in which the character appears. A character's hand becomes important during the grip of a fishing rod. A gait becomes important during a stroll down a boulevard. The face becomes important just before a kiss.

Take, for instance, the physical description of Brett Ashley as she appears in *The Sun Also Rises*. As a fine example of moving from a broad description to a specific one, Jake Barnes first proclaims Brett to be "damned good-looking." How does he define good looking? At first it's in the style of her clothing, the cut of her hair: "a slipover jersey sweater" and "a tweed skirt," her hair "brushed back like a boy's." And in case you miss the importance of Brett's fashion sense, Jake tells you that in looking at the curve of her body beneath "you missed none of it with that wool jersey."[110]

But just as readers can learn the background of a character throughout a plot—not only through a heavily frontloaded exposition in the opening act—so too can a character's description be metered out in the story. It's not until the following chapter that we have a close description of Brett's face, for instance. Only then do the details of her white face and the slope of her long neck, passing through the lights of Parisian shops, become important. It's the first time that Jake and Brett kiss. The full physical description of Brett is held back until this kiss, this moment that tells readers something of the affair between the two characters. Piece by piece, details of the character's description come into being.

In appreciating the lightness of Hemingway's style, though, we should notice that after this moment, physical details about Brett's appearance in the novel become sparse. Even as native Pamplonans scrutinize her walking by or when Jake collects her from a hotel room, crying after Romero has left her, Hemingway holds back any physical detail of Brett's changing appearance. Description established, it's through dialogue that Papa carries her characterization.

Establishing Character Description and Moving to Dialogue

Nick Adams may have thought that people were easy, particularly once a writer learns to use dialogue to make them live. But before his stories moved into dialogue on its own, Hemingway still often established characters with a type of anchor description that then moved into how they spoke to one another.

Let's look at how Hemingway describes two key characters of "The Short Happy Life of Francis Macomber." One of Papa's African stories, the plot opens with Macomber, a wealthy coward, having just been carried back to his tent in celebration of shooting a lion. But when the wounded lion had charged, Macomber ran in terror, relying upon his professional guide, Robert Wilson, to kill it. The first physical description we have of the two men comes as Margot, Macomber's wife of eleven years, looks at them both for what seems to her like the first time.

With one character, Wilson, Hemingway provides a case study in *showing* readers the physical details of the hunter's presence. With the second character, Macomber, Hemingway describes the man by *telling* readers about his social accomplishments and how others perceive him. The difference in technique is both intentional and effective in presenting them the way Papa wished.

Wilson is described as "middle height with sandy hair, a stubby mustache, a very red face and extremely cold blue eyes with faint white wrinkles at the corners that grooved merrily when he smiled." Margot glances over Wilson's body, taking in his "loose tunic," "big brown hands," "old slacks," and "very dirty boots." Hemingway's portrait of Wilson follows a classical technique known as the descending description. It starts with a character's hair and works down the face, then body. The action of the description comes from the movement of Margot's gaze over the hunter.

What Is Said and What Isn't

Literary critics and essays written for an English class might note the raw physicality in Wilson's description. Margot's vision seems charged by the ammunition he wears around his chest, "four big cartridges" ready to go off. And the descending technique has a history of sexual connotations, as in John Donne's "To His Mistress Going to Bed." But as a writer grounded in the truth of the physical rather than the symbolic, Hemingway avoids such implications in his description. If the cartridges are a sign of Wilson's sexuality, that's a hidden part of the iceberg to be left to the reader's imagination. The description, following Papa's objective method, provides only what details can be seen. Hemingway caps off what might otherwise be a caricatural description with the delightful detail of the impression left by the brim of Wilson's Stetson hat, a "white line" that limits the "baked red of his face."[111]

Macomber, as his wife sees him, was "very tall, very well built if you did not mind that length of bone, dark, his hair cropped like an oarsman, rather thin-lipped, and was considered handsome." Note the difference between this description and the first sentence in the description of Wilson. While at first glance Macomber's description may seem to have similar details—height, build, hair, mouth—they are scattered and vaguer than those given for the hunting guide. We jump from height to build to hair to mouth. We don't know exactly how "tall" or what "well built" necessarily means, certainly not to the detailed extent we see of Wilson.

Our first reading of Macomber makes him seem less authentic and more like something other than he is. His haircut isn't even his own but that of an oarsman. His safari clothing mimics Wilson's, only standing out because it looks new. It's telling that Margot thinks her husband is "considered handsome," but apparently by other people and not herself. The characterization we have of Macomber comes from Hemingway's narrator who tells us how invested he is in social niceties, controlled court games, and trophy fishing contests.[112] Since Macomber invests so much of himself in social graces, it's doubly cutting that he shows himself to be a coward "very publicly" by running from the lion.

In any meaningful sense of descriptive writing, Macomber is less physically present on the page than Wilson is. Wilson is all sun-burnt flesh, red and worn. Macomber is a wrongheaded celebration in misplaced clothing. Based on these descriptions, is it any wonder that Margot cuckolds her husband with Wilson? Is it any wonder Wilson ends up shot, a fate Margot delivers for him? Those turns of plot are believable, in part, because they begin with Hemingway's description of the characters.

Exercise: Embodying Character and Habit

Select a character for whom you've completed a profile in Chapter 3. Identify one word that most typifies that character as a person: lazy, brave, punctual, cowardly, effete. Then, in one or two paragraphs, write a physical description of the character that captures that trait. Do not use the word that typifies the character in your description. How does the voice, the hair, the weathering of face show up on a person who's lazy? Can you convey a sense of cowardliness based upon physical description alone, without overtly stating this effect to your readers?

What's the Point? Showing a character's habits and personality as part of her physical description creates a much more believable presence in your writing. To strike a reader's imagination, you need to hit the physical details that convey a sense of personality.

Mimicking Hemingway: Setting the Journey

Hemingway based "Big Two-Hearted River" on a fishing trip he took to the Fox River in the summer of 1919. Just returned from World War I, he was joined by two friends, Jock Pentecost and Al Walker, and early manuscripts of the story show that Hemingway had planned to include a group of characters. The finished version, however, isolated Nick Adams on a lone journey.

Write a story based on a trip that you've taken, a journey where you either got away from something disturbing you or learned something new about yourself. Craft the setting to suggest a connection with that internal landscape, but don't explicitly state it. Remember that you're inventing the setting, so a strict fidelity to the actual place isn't necessary.

The Snows of a Setting

Read "The Snows of Kilimanjaro" and "An Alpine Idyll," one story that leads up to mountain snowpack and another story that comes down from it. Notice how Hemingway contrasts a description of the snow against the grassy plains in "Kilimanjaro" and then against a small-town tavern in "Idyll." Write a scene in a snow-filled setting that contrasts the frozen white outside with another element—perhaps the inside of a ski lodge or house or the confined space of a car. How do your characters behave differently in each setting? Hunched over, shoulder's pinched upward in the cold? Pulling close to each other indoors to spark some warmth?

A Hotel of Differences

In "The Capital of the World," Hemingway uses a hotel for his setting, a classical device that can believably bring together a cast of characters. The setting allows the brash waiter Paco to imitate the glory of the older matadors in a tragic meeting with a counterfeit bull. Write a story set in a hotel or similar place that allows you to bring together people from different backgrounds and ages. How do characters of different ages, sexes, or professions see this same setting?

For Whom the Story's Told:
Plotted Fictions

6

"If you have a story it is not hard to tell.
Maybe people won't believe it. But you
can tell it straight and true."

(Hemingway, Letter to Charles Scribner, 4 October 1949[113])

The success that Hemingway found with his novels and short stories of the 1920s cemented his reputation as an innovator of style, description, and dialogue. In his later writing, he certainly worked at refining these elements, but the work was more a honing of impressionistic description or the cadences of speech rather than reinventing new approaches to them. When it came to narrative, however, Hemingway continuously experimented with changes in dramatic structure and perspective over the course of his life.

From the 1930s through the 1950s, Papa attempted a range of different approaches in how he shaped the events of a story and the narrative perspectives that conveyed them. Books such as *Death in the Afternoon* and *Green Hills of Africa* brought his first-person point of view techniques into nonfiction, describing the Spanish bullfight and the African safari. Works such as *For Whom the Bell Tolls* represented a departure from the Hemingway heroes who exclusively tell their own stories through detached and ironic voices.

In this chapter, we'll examine the patterns of narration that sketched Hemingway's stories into being and the points of view that colored them into life.We'll contrast the narration in Papa's classically dramatic *A Farewell to Arms* with the experimentally modern "The Snows of Kilimanjaro." We'll chart the range of perspectives Papa adopted in point of view over the course of his writing career, a willingness for experimentation that climaxed with *To Have and Have Not*.

For Whom Is the Story Told?

While revising the publishing draft of *For Whom the Bell Tolls*, Hemingway complained to Maxwell Perkins about his frequent conflicts with literary critics. Critics, he felt, too often read his work with an expectation for something that wasn't there. This left them unable to see the literary value of his decisions as a writer. "I don't like to write like God," Papa explained. "It is only because you never do it, though, that critics think you can't do it."[114]

As a statement on narration and point of view, Hemingway links his views of succinct style and direct description with the way stories create an impression upon a reader. Hemingway contrasted his style with the expansive narration found in Tolstoy. The epics of *Anna Karenina* and *War and Peace*, which play out on a national stage, boom with the all-knowing voice of God that seemingly echoes throughout all Russia. Hemingway's stories, however, most often convey a sense of a great world from a limited perspective. This was due to Papa's artistic decision, not a lack of artistic talent. As he explained to Perkins: "I can write it like Tolstoi and make the book seem larger, wiser, and all the rest of it. But then I remember that was what I always skipped in Tolstoi."[115]

The difference in narration between Tolstoy and Hemingway is the difference between the panoramic painting and the cyclorama. In *Anna Karenina*, for instance, Tolstoy follows multiple characters through a removed narrator, withdrawn from the events but able to swoop down and describe them in detail. He changes the novel's voice to fit Anna's romantic moods and her distempered ones, her lover Vronsky's honorable weaknesses, or her counterpart Levin's philosophies and happiness. The effect is of the panorama, a painting that spreads out flat against a wall to give a bird's-eye view of all events, all characters, all at once. Tolstoy tells his story as he imagines God might.

In Hemingway, however, narration is meant to mimic the cyclorama, a 360-degree painting that wraps around a circular wall to give spectators the impression that they stand in the middle of a historical reality. The goal is to create the illusion in language that readers experience the events of a story as they are reading them. Hoping to justify to his father the events that he wrote about—subjects not exactly suited to polite, middle-class Illinois—a young Hemingway explained that he wanted "not to just depict life" but to "actually make it alive."[116]

In decisions about what events to narrate and what perspective to use in telling them, it's important to keep in mind the effect a story should have upon a reader. This requires the seeding of anticipation early on and the bloom of expectation as a story progresses. All good writing takes readers into account. But in creative writing—whether fiction or nonfiction—the emphasis needs to be on how readers are caught up and carried along by a story. Leave the imperative to report events factually to newspaper columnists and historians.

When following Hemingway's style, you should leave your readers with the impression that they stand in the midst of a story's events, not that they hover above, peeking down on them.

Inventing the Story, Not Recounting Events

Some readers of *A Farewell to Arms* mistakenly assume that the novel is chiefly autobiographical, a roman à clef that fictionalizes Papa's World War I experience. Such readers imagine Frederic Henry as the stand in for Hemingway, since both character and author were injured along the Italian front. They imagine Catherine Barkley substituting for Agnes von Kurowsky, both nurses on the nightshift who become the love object of a young

American abroad. Yet, understanding *A Farewell to Arms* as a narrow reproduction of Papa's life does a serious disservice to his skill as a writer. And doing so blinds us to understanding how he invented and shaped the novel's narrative.

For this reason, Papa did not want his publisher to use his biography to promote *A Farewell to Arms*. He wanted the novel to be understood and respected for the fiction that it was. There are, then, significant differences between the artistic work and Hemingway's life. The action of *A Farewell to Arms* centers around the Italian retreat during the October 1917 Caporetto offensive. Far from experiencing that battle, Hemingway was just then beginning his stint as a reporter in Kansas City. He didn't start his service in the Italian Red Cross until the following summer.

The love affair between Frederic and Catherine also takes a different turn from the path followed by Hemingway and Agnes. Catherine shows more interest in Frederic than in his Italian friend, Rinaldi. After they fall in love in Milan while Frederic heals from his battle wounds, the two flee the war together, only to suffer a tragic end in Switzerland. Agnes, by contrast, rejected Hemingway for an Italian officer. After their Milanese romance, Agnes broke off their engagement via a letter while Hemingway waited for her in America.

To write convincingly about events he had never seen, places he had never been, Hemingway researched maps, newspapers, and books for the necessary detail. And it would be naive to think that Hemingway discounted his own experiences while fictionalizing the war. He certainly drew upon what had happened to him and the stories he had been told in crafting the novel's characters and events.

But where reality left off, the shape of the novel was determined by the writer's ability to invent a narrative—to create the war and the romance as fiction.

When Anything Can Happen in a Fiction, What Should Happen?

Hemingway's novels and short stories are not known especially for their plots. Considering Papa's influence on other aspects of American writing, it may be surprising that the author of machismo action—of battles, of bullfights, of deep-sea fishing— so downplays the importance of action in a story.

As we've seen in "The Killers," it's very often dialogue in Hemingway that takes the place of an action-oriented plot. In works such as "A Clean, Well-Lighted Place" or "Hills Like White Elephants," the quipped exchanges between characters and the ordering of a drink or three is all the plot that's needed. Even in more plot-driven stories such as "The Short Happy Life of Francis Macomber" (about a couple's encounter with a lion on safari) or "The Capital of the World" (about a Spanish waiter who tries to prove himself, matador-style, against a charging, knife-laden chair), the focus remains on the anxieties of characters and their conflicts with each other.

Hemingway's privileging of character over plot was certainly part of a larger trend in twentieth-century literature, with the exception of popular page-turners like the hard-boiled detective or romance genres. That doesn't mean that you can ignore plot, however, in styling yourself after Papa's example. Even the most character-intensive narrative must have a plot that reveals the character to us in an effective manner.

For this reason, Hemingway's plots (and most satisfying plots, for that matter) focus around character conflicts. At their most abstract level, the typical Hemingway novel poses a series of challenges to the "code hero," testing whether he can maintain his cool in the face of life's absurdities and letdowns. The disillusionments of war, the disappointments of love, the despair of death all threaten his resolve. The purpose of the plot in such a prototypical Hemingway tale is to raise the hope that heroism can survive the modern world, then to display the character's reaction as the promise of such idealism fades.

A story where a character's convictions are never tested is rarely worth reading. If Ahab were to kill the whale a week after setting sail, *Moby Dick* would be a catalog of whaling techniques, not a novel about the lengths of single-minded obsession. If Hamlet were to murder Claudius upon first seeing him, the play would lose the tension over his sanity and ability to take vengeance. If Frederic Henry were to serve bravely throughout the Italian war, rescuing the lives of wounded soldiers one after the other, and then marry Catherine and raise a family in some ticky-tacky suburb, we would lose the dramatic tensions that so engage us as readers. Drama would become melodrama.

What Happens, When, and Why: The Basics of Plot

When you ask people what a novel or film is "about," they're most likely to give you a plot summary: A character arrives in Podunk, America, robs a bank, and steals off with someone's bride. Left behind, the jilted groom takes to the drink out of losing his love, but finds consolation in a jukebox playing a Billie Holiday song. Meanwhile—back in Big City, USA—the former fiancée dumps her criminal because his bank money runs out. He wallows in depression as Billie's voice comes over the radio.

Act A leads to Consequence B, which brings about Act C, and so on.

In its most basic form, "plot" refers to the arrangement of events as they are described in a narrative. "Plot" differs in this way from the "story," a distinction made by E. M. Forster in *Aspects of the Novel*. "Story," then, is the sequence of events as they happen in time. "Plot" is a selection of deeds and their consequences, a linking together of causes and effects. "Story" is a chronology of occurrences, a bland list of what happens. "Plot" is a consequence of artistic decision, "story" a consequence of physics.

A writer using a drastically different plot structure that does not follow the sequence of a story used to be rare. Today, however, we've become accustomed to such differences in plot and story, not only in writing but also in TV shows and movies. Flashback scenes and flashforwards have become common devices for bringing an audience along a plot structure that differs from a chronology.

The distinction between "plot" and "story" is important because it gives writers a role in making decisions about what happens in the tales they tell. It's important because a writer who has developed a sense of "plot" has developed a sense of how the unfolding of events in a narrative will affect readers.

It might be easier to think of "plot" in its sense of "graph" or "chart." If you map out the events of a narrative on a chart, you can arrange and rearrange them in any order that you like. You might, for instance, begin your story with a failed criminal listening to a Billie Holiday song, and then backtrack to explain why he seems so affected by her voice.

With plot as something you can mold and remold, you can decide to leave out events that aren't central to your narrative. Hemingway did as much at the beginning of *A Farewell to Arms* when Frederic Henry takes leave from the front at the beginning of winter for a tour of Italian cities. Chapter 2 ends with his friend Rinaldi persuading him to chase women in Naples. And a priest offers to write a letter of invitation so Frederic can visit his family in the Abruzzi. At the beginning of Chapter 3, Frederic returns in early spring to apologize to the priest for not visiting his family, but pleases Rinaldi with the promise of romantic adventure. The details of Frederic's several-months absence from the front—an element of the "story," but not of the "plot"—goes unnarrated in the gap between chapters.

Hemingway's Iceberg Theory applies, then, to plot as well: the elements of the narrative seen above the water suggest aspects of the story unseen below.

So, how do you decide what should happen in a plot? Which events should be emphasized as an element of plot and which downplayed?

It's a matter of how the events you describe rise and fall in the overall arc of the narrative you're telling. By mentioning Frederic's leave, Hemingway sets up Rinaldi's character as a womanizer. This obsession with women, in turn, sets up Frederic's meeting of Catherine Barkley. As a romance, then, the narrative has little use for what Frederic did during those months in Naples, Florence, and Rome.

Exercise: A Journey into Plot

Take the longest journey that you've had, a trip during which you stopped in several places along the way. Maybe a car vacation you took across the country with your family, a road trip you took with your friends, or your walking tour of Europe. Make a list of all the places that you stopped, and arrange them in a chronological order. Then, circle only the three most interesting places that you visited; cross out all others, no matter how fascinating. If you write a series of scenes (of two to three pages each) set in those three places, ignoring those crossed out, you have a basic distinction between plot and story. You might take the memory of that journey and either narrate what happened to you in a nonfiction piece (as Papa had with *Green Hills of Africa*) or take two characters you profiled in Chapter 3 and create a fiction set in those locations.

What's the Point? Understanding the difference between plot and story is an important aspect of applying Hemingway's Iceberg Theory as a skill of narration. Omit anything that readers don't need as part of a compelling plot.

Plot: Sparking Stories Through Conflict

Our understanding of plot as the artistic structure of storytelling goes back to Aristotle. You're likely familiar with the basics of what makes for a complete story, if not from a high school or college English class, then from knowing the satisfaction that comes from reading a good novel.

As Aristotle defined it, a complete story is one that has an opening, a middle, and an end. Or, in terms of storytelling: conflict, crisis, and resolution.

Why should a story begin in conflict? Good stories most often gain the interest of readers by building anticipation over the fate of a character struggling with an acute problem. And Hemingway's stories—in a more pronounced way than most narratives—begin with and follow through on the conflicts of their characters.

Conflict, at its most basic level, refers to the struggles of a central character against some force. For readers, these competing forces set up questions that must be answered. Think for a moment about the Hemingway stories that you most admire. If a story is to grab a reader, it's likely to happen in the first few scenes or not at all.

Papa Says Frustrated over criticisms of *Green Hills of Africa*, including a letter from Scott Fitzgerald, Hemingway quipped: "If nobody can tell when a book is good why the hell write them?"[117]

Openings that engage readers most often set up a tension between people—or within one person—that needs to be resolved. In "A Clean, Well-Lighted Place," that tension has to do with an old man keeping two waiters late in a café. Will he remember to pay his bill? Why did he try to commit suicide? In *The Sun Also Rises*, that tension has to do with the competition between Jake Barnes and Robert Cohn. Why is Jake so disparaging of Robert's college boxing days? Why is the married Robert so secretive about the women they might meet? These tensions are engaging because readers want these questions answered.

Nearly all conflicts can be understood, then, as a character pitted against one of four types of forces:

1. **Against another Person**—The classical competition amongst men and women, as in *The Sun Also Rises* where Jake rivals Cohn for Brett Ashley's attention.
2. **Against Nature**—The fight against the forces of the natural world, as in *The Old Man and the Sea* where Santiago battles with an ancient marlin as old age assaults his reputation as a fisherman.
3. **Against Society**—The struggle against the institutions of humanity, as in *To Have and Have Not* where Harry smuggles to survive in a Depression economy against the interference of government bigwigs.
4. **Against the Self**—The wrestling of internal conflicts in one character, as in *A Farewell to Arms* where Frederic Henry grapples with soldierly loyalty and passionate love.

Many stories involve several of these conflicts, as *The Sun Also Rises* is equally about the struggle to find beauty—in bullfights or boxing—amidst the social changes that followed the First World War. And the typical Hemingway character of a man whose expectations for himself and his world are at odds with reality can involve any of the above. While there are narratives that emphasize character and worldly community (either in place of conflict, or in resolving conflict to make connections, as with Steinbeck's *The Grapes of Wrath*), Hemingway most often grounds his stories in the struggles of his characters. The structure of a Hemingway story, then, begins with a character's conflict and draws those struggles out in order to test the character's mettle.

If your stories begin by identifying the conflicts of a character, where do you go from there? In order to understand narrative as a complete process, we'll contrast two Hemingway stories that Papa plotted very differently. In *A Farewell to Arms* we'll see an expansion on the basic conflict-crisis-resolution pattern, one that relies upon a classical, linear form. With "The Snows of Kilimanjaro" we'll see a nonlinear plot that changes the unfolding of the story's timeline.

How Did Hemingway Generate His Stories? How Do I Generate My Own?

When asked how he came up with ideas for a fictional story, Hemingway could be quite elusive. In "Monologue to the Maestro," after the aspiring writer asks if he plans out the events of a story, Papa responded: "Almost never. I start to make it up and have happen what would have to happen as it goes along."[118]

Whether Hemingway was being coy or sincere, though, the shape of his stories shows the careful efforts of the writer as craftsman. Earlier in that same essay, Hemingway councils a distinction between the reporter's duty to describe an experience (to produce a type of written catalog of it) and the fiction writer's responsibility to create a true experience for the reader. That act of creation carries over from vivid description and honest characterization to include the act of narration that shapes events as part of the plot.

Where does the Hemingway-inspired writer get ideas for stories then? Hemingway always privileged the stories that came from experience. In an interview he gave George Plimpton, Hemingway suggested that the best training for an aspiring writer would be to hang himself because he was no good. After being cut down, he could then concentrate on being the best writer he could be: "At least he will have the story of the hanging to commence with."[119] In "Monologue to the Maestro," he offered similar advice to novices who vexed over their own abilities. Spend five years trying to write, he wrote, and if you find yourself a failure "you can just as well shoot yourself then as now."

This advice might seem glib, and portentous given Hemingway's own death. But underneath it remains two important lessons: writers should be drawing their stories from life experience, and writers must have confidence in their ability to recreate those experiences in language for readers.

Writers on Papa Robert Stone, PEN/Faulkner Award winning author of *A Flag for Sunrise* (1981), has traced Hemingway's stylistic innovations—his assembly of sentences, paragraphs—to influencing a type of morality, a cultural sense of heroic perseverance.

This doesn't mean that to write a successful story you need to speed yourself away to gritty city streets, the entrenched lines of war, or the exotic bullfighting arenas of Spain as Hemingway did. Hemingway's experiences have already been written about, after all, and they've been written about well. Your own life experiences can be the stuff of good stories yet to be told.

More practical advice, however, comes from drawing your stories from the conflicts of your characters. Hemingway often came back to the need for writers to understand how people thought and acted, and it is in characters and their complicated relations to the world that stories are made. When you're stuck and don't know what should happen in a story, or what should be emphasized or downplayed, return to the events that show us something of a character's makeup.

Give Us the Drama: Classical Narrative and *A Farewell to Arms*

In thinking about the arrangement of events in a story, you might think of readers progressing through the parts of a story as if they are watching the flight of a rocket: seeing the rocket lift from the ground, they want to know how high it will go. As it reaches its peak—the climax of its flight, caught in the tension between gravity and the thrust of its engine—they see the complexity of forces working within it. In its descent, they see the fate of those forces. If tragedy, the rocket crashes in a burst of flame and despair. If romance, the rocket floats down on a parachute of airy hope. If mystery, it disappears beyond the horizon.

So what shape does the narrative of *A Farewell to Arms* take? Papa's sentence style and radical use of dialogue distinguished him from all other writers in the English language. The story structure he used in *A Farewell to Arms*, however, is perfectly classical.

Arranged in five books, *A Farewell to Arms* follows a pattern of development common to Renaissance drama: the five-act play.

Plot and Conflict in *A Farewell to Arms*

Let's look at what happens in each book of *A Farewell to Arms*, noting the action of the plot and the character conflicts that propel our interest as readers:

Book One: Against the backdrop of the ongoing First World War, we're introduced to Frederic Henry and Catherine Barkley. Frederic's romantic desire for Catherine is sparked by his friend Rinaldi's description of her. Catherine plays into Frederic's flirtations but also resists them, perhaps out of a fear of another loss like the wartime death of her fiancé. Frederic is injured by an exploding shell.

Book Two: Following Frederic and Catherine to a Milan hospital, where Frederic heals and Catherine nurses him, we see their romance become physical. With Catherine now returning his affections, Frederic is torn from her by his duty to return to the war's front. With her lover returning to the front, Catherine reveals that she's pregnant.

Book Three: Witnessing the immense Italian retreat from Caporetto, we see Frederic's disillusionment with the war effort and the desire to keep fighting for a country not even his own. Frederic shoots a fellow Italian sergeant for running away instead of helping with a stuck ambulance. After seeing the *carabinieri* (Italian military police) execute their own officers for ordering the retreat, Frederic deserts the army by jumping into a river. Disillusioned with war and having bid his "farewell" to fighting, he plans for a life with Catherine.

Book Four: Our war-torn lovers reunited when Frederic finds Catherine in Stresa, we're now caught in an escape story when Frederic must flee Italy or face being executed for desertion. Frederic and Catherine borrow a boat and row across the lake into neutral Switzerland. Captured by the Swiss police, Frederic talks his way out of the situation by claiming they are tourists there to watch winter sports.

Book Five: With the looming promise of a "happily-ever-after" life, we hear Frederic and Catherine discuss a future touring around scenic America. Frederic wants marriage, but Catherine wants to wait until after their child is born. Tragically, Catherine's pregnancy ends in stillbirth, she dies of hemorrhaging, and Frederic can only say goodbye to her corpse.

If you've read Shakespeare's plays—say, *Hamlet* or *Macbeth*—these books of *A Farewell to Arms* should seem familiar to you. In each story, we begin with a character conflicted by competing desires: enacting revenge versus distrusting a ghostly revelation, or loyalty to king versus vaulting self-ambition. For Frederic Henry, the conflict is one between his duty to the war and his love for Cat. The events of the story, then, are designed to test the character's conflict, to play it out.

Fiction is not an account of "what's likely to happen"; it's an orchestration of dramatic elements. (And even in nonfiction, a writer must decide when to begin a story, which elements to include, which to leave out. Nonfiction is not an account of everything that really happened.) Remember that Papa is inventing what happens to Frederick and Catherine, consciously timing the announcement of Cat's pregnancy just before the Caporetto retreat.

The way in which a dramatic story develops was most carefully described by Gustav Freytag, a nineteenth-century German novelist and playwright. What is commonly known today as "Freytag's pyramid" accounts for the stages of development that correspond with the stages of Hemingway's novel. Building upon Aristotle's basic three-part structure of storytelling, Freytag's model expanded the ways in which classical narratives structured their audience's expectations.

Narrative Technique In medias res (in the middle of things) is an opening strategy used by writers to begin a story while an action is ongoing. Like *The Illiad* opening with Achilles already laying siege to Troy, *A Farewell to Arms* opens with Frederic amidst the ongoing battles of the First World War. The effect generates a sense that the narrative world of a story is greater than the plot being told.

The Dramatic Story in *A Farewell to Arms*

Let's look at each of these stages of the dramatic story using Freytag's pyramid, and see how the events of *A Farewell to Arms* move the story along or bring it to a conclusion:

1. **Exposition.** The introduction should situate readers in the world of the narrative, establishing basics such as setting and character conflict, and introduce the dramatic tensions working against the characters. This stage closes with the "activating incident," the event that sets in motion the struggles of the character.

   - In *A Farewell to Arms*, Frederic's duty as a soldier and his love for Catherine pull him in separate directions. The "activating incident" is Frederick's wounding, which makes it possible for Catherine to nurse him (as she couldn't nurse her dead fiancé) and for the couple to fall in love.

2. **Rising Action.** The second stage of a story should heighten character conflict sprung from the activating incident. Events should bring into stern relief the forces that divide a character. This stage introduces an overwhelming obstacle that compels characters to confront their conflicts, rather than narrowly skirt around them.

- In *A Farewell to Arms*, Frederic sees a life he could have with Catherine as they live in Milan. Cat's pregnancy and the call to report back to the front, however, divides Frederick's loyalties, trapping him between two desires.

3. **Climax.** The climax of a story is the cauldron of dramatic pressure. It's the moment when characters must decide how to deal with the forces dividing them, the moment when they must act to resolve the divided forces working against them.

   - Frederic's actions during the Caporetto retreat become the turning point of the conflict between war and love. In shooting the Italian sergeant for desertion but then deserting the war himself, Frederic's disillusionment with battlefield bravery is complete. He commits himself instead to his love for Cat.

4. **Falling Action.** As the activating incident brings about the rising action, the turning point of the climax spurs on the falling action of the story. Traditionally, the falling action emphasizes the forces that a character has turned against, building suspense about the character's fate and the wisdom of the turning point.

   - Frederic and Catherine's idyllic time together in Stresa, an Italian town, may seem an odd setting for a story's falling action. But as Frederic settles in with Cat and fishes at the lake, the Stresa passage serves as a counterpoint to Book II where the couple first built their relationship in Milan. Then, the war called Frederic back to the front as part of the rising action, and now the consequences of abandoning the front compel Frederic to flee when Count Greffi warns him that Italian authorities will summarily execute him if they find him.

5. **Resolution.** A story's conclusion settles the dramatic tensions it has stirred up. In tragedy, the resolution results in catastrophe, brought about in classic drama by a character's own actions—think Oedipus or Hamlet here. In romance, the resolution results in harmony, as where two lovers separated by family, friends, or society are finally brought together.

- *A Farewell to Arms* unknots the tensions threatening to divide Frederic and Catherine by delivering them to Swiss tranquility. The novel is not romantic, however, and the hope of life represented in their love is destroyed with the death of Catherine and her stillborn child.

Hemingway and the Critical Flop Despite the respect he gained from early novels such as *A Farewell to Arms*, or perhaps because of it, Hemingway's later books could draw the harsh judgment of literary critics. *Across the River and Into the Trees* (1950) experimented in plot by compressing the narrative's present to the last days of the dying central character's life. The novel invited so much scorn that it became fashionable to dismiss Papa as a fallen great. Fellow writer, Evelyn Waugh, however, rushed to Papa's defense. And *The Old Man and the Sea* (1952) would restore Hemingway's critical reputation.

Hemingway Adapts the Classical Form

Why did Hemingway use such a classical narrative form in *A Farewell to Arms*? Papa's previous novel, *The Sun Also Rises*, showed the aftermath of the Great War upon the generation that lived in its wake. *A Farewell to Arms* was his artistic treatment of the war itself. The novel presents the conflict of love amidst war as an all-transforming force, leading a conventional hero to abandon frontline bravado for romantic love. It presents Frederic as the American answer to Homer's Achilles, Shakespeare's Romeo, or Tolstoy's Pierre Bezukhov.

But Hemingway was not merely reproducing the classical form. He worked within a classical structure to adapt it to the story he was telling, a story written in and about the twentieth century.

An important difference in *A Farewell to Arms* from the classical narrative structure, for instance, has to do with Frederic's role in bringing about the story's tragic end. In the classical structure, the central character's actions during the climax bring about the story's final consequences. Thus, Hamlet's decision not to kill Claudius while praying leads to his blindly stabbing Polonius, an act that brings about his own death.

In *A Farewell to Arms*, however, Frederic's actions in Book Three—his abandoning of the war—do not directly bring about Catherine's death. Catherine is already pregnant before Frederic returns to the front, and there's no suggestion that she would have lived if he had stayed. Also, the tragedy of the novel is not Catherine's death on its own, but rather the loss of the love she shared with Frederic. In this case, Frederic's commitment to their relationship sets up the very object that her death takes away.

The lesson for any writer is to look at models for how they can offer you a platform upon which to stage your story, whether that model comes from classical drama or from Hemingway's work. Don't, however, feel constrained to that form, needing to complete it as an employee filling in a job application.

In thinking about what happens in each part of a story, you need to train yourself not to see them as events that happen spontaneously. You should train yourself to think of each story element the way you would think of each step of a staircase: each is a platform to get your characters where they need to be.

After reading the drafted manuscript of *A Farewell to Arms*, Maxwell Perkins explained to Hemingway that he should have as much time as necessary to complete his revisions. Any book that could so affect people after several readings ought to be honed as best as the artist can, Perkins thought. He wrote Hemingway with some suggestions from his own reading, however, to improve the story, the principal one having to do with the absence of the war in the second part of the novel.

A story of war in the first half, a story of love in the second, the presence of the war quietly fades away as Frederic and Catherine leave for Switzerland. Perkins felt the diminished role of the war was appropriate: two lovers so absorbed in their own emotions might believably forget the raging world outside. But Perkins also thought that the novel might close by suggesting the war had brought about Catherine's death. If the doctor would mention as much, casually, as Catherine lay dying, the effect would be one of suturing together the first and second halves of the story into a completed bundle.

Hemingway did not take Perkins's suggestion. As published, *A Farewell to Arms* is the story of love brought together in war, but torn apart by death in childbirth. The narrative structure follows Frederic's bravery in abandoning the war, then Catherine's bravery as she faces death.

Exercise: Climax and Conflict

Take two central characters that you profiled in Chapter 3, ideally a protagonist and antagonist whose motives are at cross purposes. Or, if you're stuck for ideas, imagine a teenager who has enlisted to go off to war and a mother who doesn't want him to go. Imagine a circumstance where both of these characters' desires come into immediate conflict, perhaps at the bus stop where the son is leaving to report to duty. Begin writing this conflict scene as a climax, in maybe two to three pages. After you've sketched the scene, trace back the conflict to an event that causes the conflict to come about—perhaps the moment that inspired the teenager to enlist. Then, chart ahead to how you might resolve the tensions between mother and son, perhaps in their first letters to each other while apart.

What's the Point? The classical five-act arrangement provides an effective framework for a plot that will engage and hold your readers' emotions through the arc of a narrative. By focusing on your characters' conflicts and a circumstance that brings them into relief, you'll have a sense of the climax that your story moves toward and away from.

The Story as Fragmented Shell: A Nonlinear Narrative and "The Snows of Kilimanjaro"

Though the well-formed architecture of the five-act storyline served Hemingway well in novels such as *A Farewell to Arms*, Papa also used plots that did not progress in sync with their stories. This nonlinear plot development, which jumps around in time, was used to great effect in "The Snows of Kilimanjaro."

Literary Terms "Stream of Consciousness" refers to a literary technique representing the rush of a character's internal thoughts and perceptions of the world. The success of James Joyce's *Ulysses* made the technique widespread amongst twentieth-century writers. The term was popularized by psychologist William James, who suggested that humans think more in a fragmented series of thoughts, rather than a logical pattern.

To see how Hemingway deviated from the classical dramatic structure he favored in his earlier novels, let's examine the plot of "The Snows of Kilimanjaro." Its more complex architecture blends moments of a narrative present, taking place in Africa, with the stream-of-consciousness memories (or internal monologues) of its central character. Now among Papa's most widely read stories, it was first published in 1936, a year after *Green Hills of Africa* provided a nonfiction account of the safari plains and looming mountains. Its plot moves between a narrative present and a series of *stream-of-consciousness* recollections.

Narrative Present 1: The plot begins in Africa. A writer, Harry, lies on a cot, dying of gangrene from a thorn scratch. His wife, Helen, asks him not to drink. As they quarrel, Harry imagines the stories he won't live to write.

Stream of Consciousness 1 (in italics): Harry remembers the Karagatch railway station and moments from the

Greco-Turkish War, the snow-covered mountains of Bulgaria (where he sheltered a deserter), and skiing in Austrian mountains. He has never written about any of these experiences.

Narrative Present 2: Harry castigates his wife for the luxury her wealth has brought them. After waking in the evening, Harry finds that Helen has gone hunting. While she is gone, Harry thinks over how he came to waste his skill as a writer, living in comfort rather than using his talent. Helen returns, having shot a ram for them to eat. Their quarreling turns to more pleasant exchanges about sex and the hopeful salvation of a plane, and they drink whiskey-sodas together. A hyena arrives at the edge of camp and with it Harry's acceptance that he is going to die.

Stream of Consciousness 2 (in italics): Harry thinks of Constantinople, remembering his whoring about, bickering with old lovers, and fighting with their jilted dates. He remembers the opium-producing poppy fields of Turkey and seeing dead soldiers in their white shirts and pomponed shoes. He thinks of Parisian cafés and meeting with writers such as Tristan Tzara, a founder of the Dadaist movement.

Narrative Present 3: Harry drinks the broth that Helen provides. He promises himself that he won't quarrel with her anymore, but imagines he might ruin that promise too. Harry wants to write, but Helen can't take dictation, and besides there isn't time enough. Harry imagines he might be able to get all he wanted to write into just one paragraph if he "could get it right."[120]

Stream of Consciousness 3 (in italics): Harry remembers his grandfather's hunting cabin that had been burned down and rebuilt. His grandfather's rifles, lost in the fire, were never replaced, and he never hunted again. Harry remembers fishing in Germany's Black Forest after the First World War and the Parisian apartment he had rented to use as a place to write.

Narrative Present 4: Helen wants Harry to drink more broth, but he asks for a whiskey-soda. Harry imagines he can have as much whiskey as there is after she leaves. He thinks death must be delayed on another street.

Stream of Consciousness 4 (in italics): Harry realizes that he never wrote about Paris. He remembers another story that he had intended to write but never did—a story about a ranch chore boy, beaten by the "old bastard" for whom he worked, who had shot the man dead when he tried to beat him again.[121] The memory ends with Harry wondering to himself why he never wrote down the story.

Narrative Present 5: Harry tells Helen to "tell them why," referring to the parting question about why he never wrote the stories he intended to. She can't possibly know what he means. Harry resolves that he will not worry about death, since doing so won't allow it to hurt him.

Stream of Consciousness 5 (in italics): Harry remembers Williamson, a soldier with his guts blown out after being wounded by a German grenade. Williamson begged Harry to kill him. Harry gives him all of the morphine tablets he had saved in case he needed them himself. Harry does not mention that he wished to write about Williamson's death.

Narrative Present 6: Harry has become bored with dying, but tells Helen that he had been writing before becoming too tired. Feeling death come in the vision of a hyena, Harry feels its weight press upon his chest so that he cannot breathe.

Stream of Consciousness 6 (not in italics): A plane arrives to take Harry to a hospital. After it lifts off, Harry watches zebras and wildebeests diminish on the African plains below. As they disappear into the rain clouds above, Harry catches a glimpse of the snow-packed summit of Kilimanjaro and knows that that is where he is headed.

Narrative Present 7: At their camp, Helen awakens from the crying sounds of a hyena. In their tent, she finds Harry has died, the dressings on his leg having fallen off.

If you read only the narrative "present" of the story (skipping Harry's imaginings, the sections marked in italics), you have a rather straightforward, classic narrative. The conflict of these sections, which all take place on the African plains, centers around Harry and Helen's relationship. It's not until we focus on the stream-of-consciousness moments that the story takes on a rather different conflict: Harry's inner conflicts over the life of luxury and laziness he has led with Helen versus his talents and hopes as a writer.

Papa's Influences Hemingway's literary debt for "The Snows of Kilimanjaro" largely belongs to Leo Tolstoy's "The Death of Ivan Ilyich." Both stories recount the last days of a character who treats his family with contempt, witnesses symbolic visions of death (a black sack or a hyena), and wastes away under a malodorous disease.

Plot and Conflict

At first, the story's narrative conflict might seem to be whether Harry will live or die. But as so often in Hemingway, the opening scenes of dialogue set up tensions over how characters treat one another amid danger or despair. Will Harry continue to be cruel to Helen? Will Helen find something that will make Harry want to live? The "activating incident" of the story, when read this way, occurs when Harry tells his wife that he has never loved her. The climax of the narrative present, then, comes with Harry accepting that he is going to die, but also his realization that Helen does love him even if he doesn't love her. The turning point is Harry's decision not to injure his wife further, returning to the "bread and butter" lie of pretending to love her that has sustained him all his life.[122] Resolution comes with Helen's waking up to her husband dead in the tent beside her, the hyena baying outside.

Habits of Hemingway When "The Snows of Kilimanjaro" was first published in *Esquire* magazine in August 1936, Papa included one of his customary jabs at fellow writer F. Scott Fitzgerald. Hemingway felt that Scott had wasted his talent in idolizing the wealthy. The joke in the story that the rich are different from the poor—they've got more dough—was a blow to one of Fitzgerald's openings. After Fitzgerald objected to being named in the story, future versions were printed with "Julian" in its place. ("Julian" was the name of Fitzgerald's hero in "A New Leaf," a character he largely modeled on himself.)

But in plotting "The Snows of Kilimanjaro," Hemingway complicated this straightforward narrative by interjecting the memories and unrealized stories that Harry dwells upon from his cot. With these memories added in, the central conflict of the story is not Harry and Helen's relationship with each other. The central conflict rests within Harry's own consciousness. It becomes Harry's struggle in accepting his own death while coming to terms with the stories that he won't live long enough to write, and his failure as an artist for not having written them sooner.

The "activating incident" in Harry's conflict with himself as a writer, then, is his realization that time has grown too short to finish his work, an understanding that occurs to him at the end of the first scene in the narrative present. As the passel of stories that he could have written grows (over the stream-of-consciousness segments), the climax comes with his resolve to set things right with one, true paragraph. Given the futility of that gesture, the dramatic tension resolves itself with a story that shouldn't be written, the death of Williamson.

First-time readers encountering the last stream-of-consciousness episode may hope that Harry has indeed been saved. After all, the lack of italics suggests that the flight to Kilimanjaro is real, not solely Harry's subjective experience. But this final moment of Harry's vision—he has died at the end of Narrative Present 6, the hyena's weight risen from his chest—comes as his last story to us. A fitting dénouement to how the failed writer of Austrian snow-covered peaks will be remembered as part of Africa's tallest summit.

Hemingway uses this nonlinear structure as a way of complicating the character conflicts and narrative experience for his readers. The dramatic arc of a story about a feuding marriage at the brink of the husband's death merges with the lifetime aspirations of a writer's dying regrets. The structure allows for a much more detailed exposition of Harry's character, revealing his past throughout the entire story, not only in its opening act. His stream-of-consciousness memories, while describing events locked in the story's past, align alongside other plot elements to explain his interactions with Helen in the present.

Exercise: Picking Out Plot

Select three of Hemingway's plots—either short stories or novels—and examine the events that shape their narratives. Chart out the sequence of events in each. Can you group the scenes of the story into clear divisions? (Five acts? Three acts?) Do the stories contain an "activating incident"? A climactic turning point? A satisfactory resolution?

Hemingway's Plots
Story
Activating Incident
Climax
Resolution

What's the Point? In mapping out how Hemingway planned his stories, you should begin to get the feel of what makes for a complete story—the steps that move readers from beginning to middle to end.

Exercise: Plot and Character Conflict

For the three stories you charted in the previous exercise, ask yourself what situation characters are placed in by the events of each act. Do particular plot events force characters to make decisions about their conflicted interests? Do events highlight the tensions dividing a character? How do these events relate to the conflicts (internal and external) that a character has? Do characters' actions seem to bring about what happens to them? Or do events seem to happen to the characters in spite of their action (or inaction)?

What's the Point? The events of a story—and how they've been arranged by the plot—should have a purpose. In this exercise, you should begin to see how those scripted events reveal something about the story's characters.

Loading the Gun: Techniques for Building Anticipation in a Story

Anton Chekov, the Russian playwright and short-story writer, explained that if a writer introduces a gun at a story's beginning it had better go off by the end. Applied to description and setting, Chekov's advice reminds writers to choose only elements that are essential to a story, not to merely offer a catalog of irrelevant detail in the hope of being realistic. What determines if an element—an object, an event, a line of dialogue—is essential?

In terms of plot and narrative, Chekov's gun reminds writers to follow through on a story's essential elements. The beginning of a story sets up a promise to readers, an expectation that readers will want to see fulfilled in completing the story.

Hemingway uses the principle of Chekov's gun in "An Alpine Idyll," a story where the narrator (unspecified but generally thought to be Nick Adams) describes the end of a month spent skiing in the Silvretta. As the narrator and his companion, John, come down from the mountains and find somewhere to drink, they mention a burial they saw while coming into town. The innkeeper explains that it was for a peasant's wife and tells them, "You wouldn't believe what just happened about that one."[123]

That phrase, "You wouldn't believe," is the sound of Papa loading Chekov's gun. The technique is simple enough. Think of the stories that a person begins with: "You're not going to believe this, but . . . " Would that person really be telling you a story that's ultimately futile, knowing that you'll dismiss whatever is said? Not likely. The preface, "you're not going to believe this," pulls listeners' interest into the tale, letting them know that there's something worth listening for.

In "An Alpine Idyll," despite the narrator and John asking to be told what happened with the peasant, the innkeeper delays, first asking where they've come from. After the church sexton joins the group, the innkeeper asks him to tell the pair what happened. But as the sexton conveys the story of the peasant's dead wife, the innkeeper continues to interrupt, telling the pair when its climax is about to come. The details presented as the story unfolds build suspense for the unbelievable—the wife had died months ago, before the mountain passes could be traveled, and her corpse was found lying across the bed, its face oddly distorted.

Why is her face misshapen? The answer to that question is the sound of the story's gun firing. Before it fires, readers are captivated, waiting to see what the peasant did to his wife. After it goes off, readers lose the dramatic impulse pulling them along. The impulse gone, Papa resolves the story with a quick exchange between the narrator and John, the innkeeper and the sexton.

Facts of Hemingway Ezra Pound suggested trimming "An Alpine Idyll" of its introduction to get to its main object. As Hemingway published it, the mystery of the peasant's wife doesn't begin until halfway through.

The principle of Chekov's gun depends upon effectively creating anticipation in the reader. When a novel is described as a real "page-turner"—a book that can't be put down until read completely through—it's likely because its narrative has baited the anticipation of its climax well, either in one overarching buildup or a series of suspenseful scenes. Often both. In tragedy, this suspense builds over the fate of the central characters. Will they survive or are they doomed? In romance, suspense builds over the love of a couple. Will they overcome the friends and family dividing them? In a mystery novel, suspense lingers over the solving of a puzzle. Will characters figure out the riddle?

Use It or Lose It

Chekov's gun also warns writers to follow through on the elements of a story. A reader's anticipation should not be built up and then abandoned. Nor should anticipation over your character's fate be too quickly cut off by an unbelievable resolution.

When a writer introduces an unused element into a narrative—a gun that never goes off—the story has a "loose end." If readers have had their expectations built up but fail to see a conflict played out, or if a story contains trumped-up details that ultimately prove meaningless, the carefully woven threads of a narrative unravel in the frayed ends of a failed story. Imagine *The Sun Also Rises* introducing Robert Cohn's experience as a boxer but never using that prowess as part of his savage beating of Romero.

By contrast, when narrative tensions are too easily resolved by an element introduced too suddenly and unexpectedly, the story relies on a technique known as *deus ex machina* (god out of the machine). Here, instead of following through on elements established earlier in the story, the unskilled writer makes up an easy way out. The carefully woven threads of narrative tension are sheared off by the unimaginative scissors of lazy storytelling. Readers are shortchanged. Imagine *A Farewell to Arms* ending not with Catherine's death in childbirth, an element established earlier by her doctor's discussion of her small waist, but by her being saved by Frederic's brother Paulie, a surgeon just flown in on vacation from Kansas City. How unappealing.

Literary Term Deus ex machina (god out of the machine): An unexpected and unsatisfactory resolution to characters' problems, *Deus ex machina* comes from ancient Greek theatre when gods would suddenly descend (via a crane) onto the stage to save characters who had found themselves in trouble over their mortal heads. In modern storytelling, it's a cheat that's to be avoided.

In the hands of skilled writers such as Hemingway, foreshadowing is a common technique often associated with the principle of Chekov's gun. Foreshadowing is a hint of events coming later in the story. The technique stacks the deck of a plot, giving readers insight into an event.

A Farewell to Arms uses foreshadowing in Chapter 8, for instance, when Frederic casually mentions his loss of a Saint Anthony necklace when he was wounded. This is the novel's first suggestion that Frederic will be injured, an event that doesn't occur in the story until Chapter 9. This use of foreshadowing is as direct as possible, a narrator telling the audience of something that will take place. Foreshadowing can be more subtle as well, as a suggestion or association of story elements with a type of event. Innumerable high school English themes have been written on the foreshadowing of rain suggesting death in *A Farewell to Arms*.

Subtlety and Silence: Building Suspense Around the Unspoken

One of Hemingway's most distinctive uses of anticipation in storytelling is the buildup of anxiety around something not explicitly stated. We've seen this work in "The Killers" where the diner crowd obeys the commands of Al and Max, but readers aren't given a description of the gangsters' guns until the end of the scene. Here, again, the iceberg within sight suggests a fuller world below. The key to this technique lies in subtlety: revealing enough so that your readers are caught up in a scene's suspense, find the moment believable, but are not forced along by heavy-handed suggestion. It's the suggestion of the whisper over the blare of the loudspeaker.

Hemingway's best-known use of the unspoken suggestion occurs in "Hills Like White Elephants." There, the couple's arguing over drinks and conversation belies the cause of the tension lying beneath—an argument over an abortion. The words "pregnant" or "abortion," however, are never mentioned in the story. Readers can only pick up what the American man is trying to pressure Jig into doing from the selective details he provides in describing the operation to her. Before that revelation, the source of the couple's anxiety draws readers into their relationship. Afterward, the tension of Jig's response pulls readers along: what will she decide, given her lover's veiled demands?

Literary critics have compared the conspicuous absence of the word "abortion" in "Hills Like White Elephants" with the similar absence of the word "homosexual" in Hemingway's "A Simple Enquiry." In the latter story, an army major, cruising after his own interest, interrogates a teenage orderly about his romantic life. The subtext of their conversation only reaches the surface when the major asks the soldier if he's "corrupt,"[124] which is as close as the story gets to stating the issue of homosexuality. (In a similar way, "operation" stands in place of "abortion" in "Hills Like White Elephants.") Both stories avoid giving name to a divisive moral topic. Doing so allows the stories to treat a contentious subject with a delayed sense of revelation, not rushing to judgment before readers can understand the characters involved.

Literary Term Vignette: A brief sketch of a story, typically only a few hundred words long. The emphasis is on economy and compression, rather than drawn-out narrative. Hemingway used a series of vignettes as interchapters between the collected short stories of *In Our Time* (1925).

The silence of "A Simple Enquiry" on the issue of homosexuality, though, has a different effect from the unstated issue in "Hills Like White Elephants" because its narrative is closer in length to a vignette than a short story. In "A Simple Enquiry," the unspoken subject gives us a quick insight into the major's character. The narrative tension does not play out, however, and the exchange's effect on the orderly is not revealed. As the orderly goes about his business, observed by the adjutant while the major sits in his office, it's clear that the subject should remain unspoken by the characters. In "Hills Like White Elephants," the unspoken subject not only provides the basis for the argument between Jig and her demanding lover, but the story also gives voice to Jig's very vocal retorts.

From Whose Point of View Is the Story Told? The Perspective of Narrative

Point of view refers to the person telling a story, its narrator. With some of Hemingway's stories, particularly in his early works, the point of view is clear and direct—a given character recounts events as he remembers them. With others, however, the narrator is less clear and may even change over the course of a single story.

There are three principal types of narration most often used in fiction:

1. **First-Person Narrator**—A narrator that participates in the story, or at least witnesses it, and uses "I" or "we."
2. **Third-Person Narrator, Limited**—A narrator removed from the story that uses "he," "she," or "they," but closely follows the actions and thoughts of one character.
3. **Third-Person Narrator, Omniscient**—An all-knowing narrator that also uses "he," "she," or "they," but can describe everything that happens in different places at the same time and often follows the actions and thoughts of several characters.

The received wisdom about different points of view is that the first-person is the most biased, the most subjective, because it filters events through a personal experience. A third-person narrator, either limited in perspective or all-knowing, isn't as seemingly objective as you might imagine. After all, it is you as the writer who decides what details to leave in or how to understand the characters and events of a story.

First-Person Bias

You can immediately grasp the presence of such first-person bias in the opening of *The Sun Also Rises* where Jake Barnes begins: "Robert Cohn was once middleweight boxing champion of Princeton. Do not think that I am very much impressed by that as a boxing title, but it meant a lot to Cohn."[125] Surely, if Cohn were to introduce himself as a character, it wouldn't be to downplay his college boxing reputation. And Hemingway made his narrator aware of his own ability to tell the story. Barnes later comments that he hasn't described Cohn well enough, explaining that he never noticed Cohn until he became his rival for Brett's affections. Thus, the opinions that the novel has about

Robert Cohn—his Jewishness, his abilities as a boxer, a writer, a lover—must be understood as the opinions of Jake Barnes.

But as a writer shaping the voice of your story, you will find the first-person invaluable in making the world come alive by the way your narrator colors it. This requires, of course, a detailed understanding of your narrating character's profile. Where is your narrator from? How old is your narrator? How would a character born ten years earlier than you—or later than you—describe the same events? Twenty years? Thirty? What life events (personal? national?) have shaped the way your narrator sees the world?

Habits of Hemingway Wyndham Lewis, a writer with whom Papa often quarreled during the Paris years, once wrote a cutting review of Hemingway's first-person singular narrators, calling them idiotic versions of the author himself. Papa was so angered by the review that he smashed one of Sylvia Beach's vases.[126]

When Hemingway relied upon first-person narrators, they were most often central characters, his "code heroes." This habit allowed Hemingway to emphasize the "code" as a way of reacting to the events of the narrative. If your narrator is secondary to the central character of your story (as Fitzgerald's Nick Carraway is to the "Great" Jay Gatsby), you'll need as detailed a sense of that character's personality, history, and conflicts as you have of your protagonist's.

Over the course of his career, Hemingway used a range of different narrators, adapting different voices to achieve the effect he wanted from a particular tale. The short stories of *In Our Time,* his 1925 collection, demonstrate some of the range Papa would use in his fiction. Most of these stories use a third-person narrator, typically linked closely to one character and most frequently Nick Adams. (By contrast, seven of the sixteen interchapters, which are rarely longer than one paragraph, rely upon a first-person narrator.) This removed, more objective narration allows a writer to stand apart from one character's singular view of the world. It also allowed Hemingway to experiment with the imagistic description and stand-alone, free-flowing dialogue that became a trademark of his style.

The three first-person stories of *In Our Time* stand out by revealing something to readers that the storytelling characters might not quite understand themselves. Two are brief but lingering scenes of character memory. In "On the Quai at Smyrna," a soldier stationed on a pier describes his absurd interactions with Turkish officers and the horrors he witnesses during the Greco-Turkish War. In "The Revolutionist," an Italian man recalls the visit of a youth chasing after the communist dream, perhaps a reminder of the narrator's own lost beliefs. "My Old Man," the most developed of the three, follows an American boy's disillusionment with the horse-racing world of his father. This last narrator, innocent and most naive, allows Hemingway to suggest most drastically that the state of the world is at odds with the mind of the narrator.

Literary Term Naive narrator: A narrator who isn't fully aware of the implications, consequences, or seriousness of the events being described, often a device of irony. Hemingway had several models he could use in crafting his own naive narrators: Mark Twain's *The Adventures of Huckleberry Finn*, Sherwood Anderson's "I'm a Fool," and Ring Lardner's *Gullible's Travels*.

In contrast to the frequent third-person narrators of *In Our Time*, Hemingway's early novels relied upon a first-person point of view. Narrators such as Jake Barnes and Frederic Henry are, not coincidentally, fictional characters who most closely resembled Hemingway's own life experience. Jake and Frederic's first-person perspective has been critical in shaping how literary critics understand the role of the "code hero" in describing a wavering world filled with wavering people. Rendered distant and impotent from a wartime injury, Jake offers a detached view of expatriate sexuality that is essential to the voice of *The Sun Also Rises*. The same events narrated from the perspective of Brett Ashley, so central to the desires of the novel's men, would take on a decidedly different flavor.

A Shifting Viewpoint

After the success of these early novels, Papa continued to experiment with different points of view in both his fiction and nonfiction works. The overall trend of his major works, however, was a shift to third-person narration, often limited to describing the inner thoughts of his central characters:

The Sun Also Rises (1926):	First Person (Jake Barnes)
A Farewell to Arms (1929):	First Person (Frederic Henry)
Death in the Afternoon (1932):	First Person, Nonfiction
Green Hills of Africa (1935):	First Person, Nonfiction
To Have and Have Not (1937):	Multiple Narrators—First Person, Varying (Harry Morgan, Albert) and Third Person, Omniscient
For Whom the Bell Tolls (1940):	Third-Person, Omniscient (But often limited to Robert Jordan's consciousness)
The Old Man and the Sea (1952):	Third Person, Limited (Santiago)

Hemingway's most radical experiment with point of view occurred in *To Have and Have Not* (1937). The novel's episodic plot and changing narration resembles Faulkner's *The Sound and the Fury* (1929) or John Dos Passos's *The Big Money* (1937) more than it does Papa's earlier novels. Harry Morgan, a charter fisherman turned smuggler, begins telling his story in the first person. One of the most problematic of Papa's "code heroes," Harry is compelled by a failing economy to smuggle people and run booze in the Atlantic waters between Cuba and Florida, but he's also both racist and murderer. The narration shifts to a third-person omniscient perspective able to describe the unuttered thoughts of both Harry and secondary characters around him. Returning to the first-person, the narration goes to Harry's deckhand Albert, then back again to Harry, and then again to the third-person.

Habits of Hemingway Like his attack on Fitzgerald as a writer in "The Snows of Kilimanjaro," Papa criticized John Dos Passos in the caricature of the effete writer Richard Gordon in *To Have and Have Not*.

Such changing points of view in *To Have and Have Not* came, in part, from the book's origin in two short stories that Papa thought worked well enough to expand into a novel. They also represented Hemingway's response to Depression-era readers who wanted a more politically aware perspective from the writer who had so effectively brought to life an earlier generation's great struggles. The novel was not well received by most critics, however, and Hemingway himself later dismissed it as a failed experiment.

Exercise: Two Sides to Any Accident

Write a scene of three to four pages in which your narrator is a woman who is struck by another car while driving. Where was she going when the accident happened? Did she secretly not want to arrive there? Was she in a hurry? Where was she coming from? What song was she listening to when it happened? Who was in the car with her? As you build up to the accident, send glass flying, and then deal with the aftermath, narrate the scene from the woman's point of view. After you're done, write another three to four pages in which you narrate the accident from the other driver's perspective, a man who, perhaps, runs a stoplight. What prevents him from stopping? Something mechanical in his car? Some anxiety about where he's going? Make this male driver significantly different (in age, personality, and class) from the woman. How can you change the voice of this second point of view by linking it to this drastically different character?

What's the Point? Hemingway often kept his point of view close to one central character in his writing, but there were occasions, as in *To Have and Have Not*, when he experimented with shifts in narrative perspective. In using different points of view for narrating the same event, you'll begin to notice how decisions about perspective can alter the effect upon your readers.

When you're deciding upon the point of view for a story, then, follow Papa's lesson by carefully considering what perspective to use and sticking with it. It can be a helpful exercise to narrate the same event from multiple perspectives—doing so allows writers settling in to a voice to see its tones by contrasting it against others. And there certainly have been successful novels that have shifted perspectives to excellent effect. (Faulkner became a master in the shifting perspective with *As I Lay Dying*, for example.) But don't vary perspectives within a story simply to show off your technical mastery. Do so carefully and only after you're certain about the effect you want to produce.

Mimicking Hemingway: The Unreliable Code

Invent an unreliable narrator, either one who's very young (as in "My Old Man") or one who has questionable motives in describing what takes place (Harry in *To Have and Have Not*). Make the character have taken as fact so many of Hemingway's stories that he believes in the Hemingway "code" as a model for life. Write a story where he tries to live out this code, despite being misguided or inept, and attempts to convince an audience that he lives up to the Hemingway ideal.

Inventing the Causes of Reality

Take one of the most dramatic moments that you've witnessed in the last month—perhaps a moment of heroism, tragedy, or fate. But even something that is perfectly banal, but has a complex human element to it, will suffice. Then imagine two events that brought this moment about, not real events but fictional ones that you consider believable and interesting. Following a scene from *The Sun Also Rises*, you may have witnessed someone's outburst, impromptu and unprovoked, before a group of friends gathered around a bar. You might select two events that explain (1) what happened that made this person was so emotional, and (2) what suggestion brought this group of friends together at that moment, at that place. Write three scenes of two to three pages each where you present the dramatic moment and both of its causes. If you rearrange the order in which you present the events, is there a different effect for readers? For instance, if you explain the reason for the outburst first and then whatever anxiety brought it about, does that make readers less or more likely to sympathize with a character breaking up the revelry of a bar?

Beneath the Elephant Iceberg

Hemingway's "Hills Like White Elephants" ends with Jig's ambiguous smile. Pressed on how she's feeling, she tells her lover that she's okay. Surely this is a return to the unexpressed frustration she felt at the beginning of the story, the bitterness at the man's callous gestures revealed only in comments about their drinks. This is as much of the iceberg's surface as Papa gives us, but you might use this as the beginning of an ongoing story. What happens with Jig after the train finally arrives? Does she board it? If so, what happens on board? Or when the couple arrives where they're going? Instead of wrapping up Hemingway's story at the train bar, write your own story that uses "Hills Like White Elephants" as its own unseen premise. After you've followed Jig's perspective, you might experiment by changing point of view to the man's side.

Writing after Hemingway: Learn to Write What Hasn't Been Done

In treading the same hills over which Hemingway passed, from Michigan to Spain, we can hope to make something of Papa's experience our own. We can hope to pick up some of the inspiration that the adventurer has left behind—perhaps in the glimpse of a stream or the echo of a couple's conversation. In reading through the stories that Hemingway wrote, about Nick Adams or the African plains, we can hope to make Papa's style our own. We can hope to stumble upon some revelation of language that the author has led us to—some word that conjures the vision of a trout or a phrase that carries the depth of a character's personality.

But repetition and variation alone do not a writer make.

In order to become the writer he wanted to be, Hemingway knew that he had to write about what hadn't yet been written. To do so, he privileged his life's experiences and observations, perhaps at the expense of imagination. The first generation of readers that found Jake Barnes and Brett Ashley compelling did so out of a belief that there was something new in their gallivanting about modern Paris and Pamplona.

Hemingway also knew that he had to write in a style that bested generations of past writers. Contemptuous of what he saw as the literary industry's need for the fashionable writer of the week, Hemingway thought of himself as competing with great writers who were still revered long after they were dead. His early success with *The Sun Also Rises*, a novel especially popular amongst the college-age crowd, may have fueled an anxiety about proving his talent was more than the vogue of just one generation. But this macho sense of writing as competition—with the past and with himself—produced a distinctive style that changed how writers of the American vernacular conceive of the way in which the printed language can work. Hemingway had his own host of influences, both contemporary and past, but he learned to take from them what was useful and fashion it into a style distinctly his own.

Your goals as a writer need not be the ability to surpass the greatest novelists of the last century. You may want only to add to the numbers of playful epigones who parody Papa for a laugh. You may want to produce one story about which you can be proud. Or you may hope to set upon a writer's career, living from published novel to published novel.

Whatever your writerly aspirations, you should understand Hemingway's techniques as a way of understanding your own sentences. You should imitate Hemingway's style as a way toward finding your own. You should follow Hemingway's well-worn track as a way of breaking off to your own originality.

Every apprentice must move beyond the master.

Notes

1. Ernest Hemingway, "Old Newsman Writes: A Letter from Cuba," in *By-Line: Ernest Hemingway* (New York: Bantam Books, 1968), 159.

2. Hemingway to F. Scott Fitzgerald, May 18, 1934, in *Ernest Hemingway: Selected Letters, 1917–1961*, ed. Carlos Baker (New York: Charles Scribner's Sons, 1981), 408.

3. Kenneth S. Lynn, *Hemingway* (New York: Simon and Schuster, 1987), 139.

4. Valerie Hemingway, "Hemingway's Cuba, Cuba's Hemingway," *Smithsonian*, August 2007.

5. Footnote. *Ernest Hemingway: Selected Letters, 1917–1961*, ed. Carlos Baker (New York: Charles Scribner's Sons, 1981), 581.

6. Maxwell Perkins to Hemingway, May 18, 1926, in *The Only Thing That Counts: The Ernest Hemingway-Maxwell Perkins Correspondence,* ed. Matthew J. Bruccoli (Columbia: University of South Carolina Press, 1996), 38.

7. Hemingway, "An Old Newsman Writes: A Letter from Cuba," in *By-Line: Ernest Hemingway,* ed. William White (New York: Charles Scribner's Sons, 1967), 155.

8. Charles A. Fenton, *The Apprenticeship of Ernest Hemingway: The Early Years* (New York: The Viking Press, 1965) 33.

9. Fenton, *The Apprentice of Ernest Hemingway: The Early Years* (New York: The Viking Press, 1965), 34.

10. Fenton, *The Apprentice of Ernest Hemingway: The Early Years* (New York: The Viking Press, 1965), 25.

11. Ernest Hemingway, "Kerensky, The Fighting Flea," *Kansas City Star,* December 16, 1917, in *Ernest Hemingway, Cub Reporter: Kansas City Star Stories*, ed. Matthew J. Bruccoli (Pittsburgh: University of Pittsburgh Press, 1970), 25.

12. Ernest Hemingway, "Mix War, Art and Dancing," *Kansas City Star,* April 21, 1918, in *Ernest Hemingway, Cub Reporter: Kansas City Star Stories*, ed. Matthew J. Bruccoli (Pittsburgh: University of Pittsburgh Press, 1970), 56.

13. Matthew J. Bruccoli, ed., *Ernest Hemingway, Cub Reporter: Kansas City Star Stories* (Pittsburgh: University of Pittsburgh Press, 1970), 56.

14. Ernest Hemingway to His Family, November 19, 1917, in *Ernest Hemingway: Selected Letters, 1917–1961,* ed. Carlos Baker (New York: Charles Scribner's Sons, 1981), 2.

15. Ernest Hemingway, "At the End of the Ambulance Run," *Kansas City Star,* January 20, 1918, in *Ernest Hemingway, Cub Reporter: Kansas City Star Stories*, ed. Matthew J. Burccoli (Pittsburgh: University of Pittsburgh Press, 1970), 32.

16. "Europe's Tragedy in Current Fiction," *The New York Times,* May 28, 1916.

17. Quoted in Joseph Hergesheimer, *Hugh Walpole: An Appreciation* (New York: George H. Doran & Company, 1919), 41.

18. Hemingway to Charles Poore, January 23, 1953, in *Ernest Hemingway: Selected Letters, 1917–1961*, ed. Carlos Baker (New York: Charles Scribner's Sons, 1981), 800.

19. Hemingway to Charles Poore, January 23, 1953, in *Ernest Hemingway: Selected Letters, 1917–1961*, ed. Carlos Baker (New York: Charles Scribner's Sons, 1981), 800.

20. Hemingway to John Dos Passos, April 22, 1925, in *Ernest Hemingway: Selected Letters, 1917–1961*, ed. Carlos Baker (New York: Charles Scribner's Sons, 1981), 157–58.

21. Hemingway to William Smith, August 5, 1925, quoted in James R. Mellow, *Hemingway: A Life without Consequences* (Cambridge, MA: Da Capo Press, 1992), 302.

22. Hemingway to Lewis Galantière, in Sherwood Anderson, *Letters*, ed. Howard Mumford Jones (Boston: Little, Brown and Company, 1953), 83.

23. Ernest Hemingway, "My Old Man," in *The Complete Short Stories of Ernest Hemingway* (New York: Charles Scribner's Sons, 2003), 157.

24. Sherwood Anderson, "I Want to Know Why," in *Sherwood Anderson: Short Stories*, ed. Maxwell Geismar (New York: Hill and Wang, 1962), 8.

25. Sherwood Anderson, *Letters,* ed. Howard Mumford Jones (Boston: Little, Brown and Company, 1953), 85.

26. Hemingway to Gertrude Stein, August 15, 1924, in *The Flowers of Friendship: Letters Written to Gertrude Stein*, ed, Donald Gallup (New York: Alfred A. Knopf, 1953), 165.

27. Ernest Hemingway, "On the Quai at Smyrna," in *The Complete Short Stories of Ernest Hemingway* (New York: Charles Scribner's Sons, 2003), 63.

28. Linda Wagner-Martin, "I Like You Less and Less: The Stein Subtext in *Death in the Afternoon*," in *A Companion to*

Hemingway's Death in the Afternoon, ed, Miriam Mandel (Rochester, NY: Camden House, 2004), 62

29. Ernest Hemingway, *A Moveable Feast* (New York: Bantam Books, 1979), 132.

30. Ezra Pound to Ernest Hemingway, December 21, 1926, JFK Presidential Library & Museum, quoted in Lynn, *Hemingway* (New York: Simon and Schuster, 1987), 167.

31. "Plimpton: Interview with Hemingway," in *Hemingway and His Critics,* ed, Carlos Baker (New York: Hill and Wang, 1961), 26.

32. Ezra Pound, "A Few Don'ts by an Imagiste." *Poetry* (1913).

33. Hemingway to Howell Jenkins, March 20, 1922, in *Ernest Hemingway: Selected Letters, 1917–1961*, ed. Carlos Baker (New York: Charles Scribner's Sons, 1981), 65.

34. Ernest Hemingway, *Death in the Afternoon* (New York: Charles Scribner's Sons, 2003), 192.

35. Ernest Hemingway, *A Moveable Feast* (New York: Bantam Books, 1979), 75.

36. Hemingway to Maxwell Perkins, March 17, 1928, in *Ernest Hemingway: Selected Letters, 1917–1961*, ed. Carlos Baker (New York: Charles Scribner's Sons, 1981), 273.

37. Hemingway to Harvey Breit, 1956, in *Ernest Hemingway: Selected Letters, 1917–1961*, ed. Carlos Baker (New York: Charles Scribner's Sons, 1981), 863.

38. Hemingway to Arthur Mizener, January 11, 1951, in *Ernest Hemingway: Selected Letters, 1917–1961*, ed. Carlos Baker (New York: Charles Scribner's Sons, 1981), 718.

39. Ernest Hemingway, "The Battler," in *The Complete Short Stories of Ernest Hemingway* (New York: Charles Scribner's Sons, 2003), 97.

40. Hemingway, *A Moveable Feast* (New York: Bantam Books, 1979), 75.

41. Hemingway to F. Scott Fitzgerald, December 24, 1925, in *Ernest Hemingway: Selected Letters, 1917–1961*, ed. Carlos Baker (New York: Charles Scribner's Sons, 1981), 181.

42. Ezra Pound, *ABC of Reading* (New York: New Directions Publishing, 1960), 29.

43. Hemingway, "The Battler," in *The Complete Short Stories of Ernest Hemingway* (New York: Charles Scribner's Sons, 2003), 98.

44. Ernest Hemingway, *Green Hills of Africa* (New York: Charles Scribner's Sons, 2003), 20.

45. Ernest Hemingway, *For Whom the Bell Tolls* (New York: Charles Scribner's Sons, 2003), 1.

46. A. E. Hotchner, *Papa Hemingway: A Personal Memoir* (New York: Da Capo Press, 2005), 69–70.

47. Ernest Hemingway, *The Sun Also Rises* (New York: Charles Scribner's Sons, 1970), 153.

48. Ernest Hemingway, *The Old Man and the Sea* (New York: Charles Scribner's Sons, 2003), 10.

49. Hemingway to Bernard Berenson, March 20, 1953, in *Ernest Hemingway: Selected Letters, 1917–1961*, ed. Carlos Baker (New York: Charles Scribner's Sons, 1981), 809.

50. Hemingway to John Dos Passos, March 26, 1932, in *Ernest Hemingway: Selected Letters, 1917–1961*, ed. Carlos Baker (New York: Charles Scribner's Sons, 1981), 354.

51. Hemingway to F. Scott Fitzgerald, April 20, 1926, in *Ernest Hemingway: Selected Letters, 1917–1961*, ed. Carlos Baker (New York: Charles Scribner's Sons, 1981), 200.

52. Hemingway, *Death in the Afternoon* (New York: Charles Scribner's Sons, 2003), 191.

53. Ernest Hemingway, *To Have and Have Not* (New York: Charles Scribner's Sons, 2003), 177.

54. Lynn, *Hemingway* (New York: Simon and Schuster, 1987), 297.

55. Baker, *Hemingway and His Critics* (New York: Hill and Wang, 1961), 33.

56. Matthew Joseph Bruccoli, ed., *The Notebooks of F. Scott Fitzgerald* (New York: Harcourt Brace, 1978), 336.

57. *By-Line: Ernest Hemingway,* ed. William White (New York: Charles Scribner's Sons, 1967), 190.

58. Carlos Baker, *Ernest Hemingway: A Life Story* (New York: Charles Scribner's Sons, 1969), 154.

59. Baker, *Hemingway and His Critics* (New York: Hill and Wang, 1961), 33.

60. Hemingway to Bernard Berenson, March 20–22, 1953, in *Ernest Hemingway: Selected Letters, 1917–1961*, ed. Carlos Baker (New York: Charles Scribner's Sons, 1981), 808.

61. Hemingway, *The Sun Also Rises* (New York: Charles Scribner's Sons, 1970), 165.

62. Hemingway, *The Sun Also Rises* (New York: Charles Scribner's Sons, 1970), 216.

63. Hemingway, *The Sun Also Rises* (New York: Charles Scribner's Sons, 1970), 22.

64. Harold Loeb, *The Way it Was* (New York: Criterion Books, 1959), 152.

65. Maxwell Perkins to Hemingway, October 30, 1926, in *The Only Thing That Counts: The Ernest Hemingway-Maxwell Perkins Correspondence,* ed. Matthew J. Bruccoli (Columbia: University of South Carolina Press, 1996), 47.

66. Hemingway to Maxwell Perkins, November 16, 1926, in *The Only Thing That Counts: The Ernest Hemingway-Maxwell*

Perkins Correspondence, ed. Matthew J. Bruccoli (Columbia: University of South Carolina Press, 1996), 48.

67. Hemingway to Maxwell Perkins, November 16, 1926, in *The Only Thing That Counts: The Ernest Hemingway-Maxwell Perkins Correspondence*, ed. Matthew J. Bruccoli (Columbia: University of South Carolina Press, 1996), 48

68. Richmond Barret, "Babes in the Bois," *Harper's Weekly*, May 1928, 727.

69. "Marital Tragedy," review of *The Sun Also Rises*, *New York Times*, October 31, 1926.

70. "Plimpton: Interview with Hemingway," in *Hemingway and His Critics*, ed. Carlos Baker (New York: Hill and Wang, 1961).

71. Hemingway to Carol Hemingway, October 5, 1929, in *Ernest Hemingway: Selected Letters, 1917–1961*, ed. Carlos Baker (New York: Charles Scribner's Sons, 1981), 308.

72. Hemingway, "The Killers," in *The Complete Short Stories of Ernest Hemingway* (New York: Charles Scribner's Sons, 2003), 218.

73. Hemingway, "The Killers," in *The Complete Short Stories of Ernest Hemingway* (New York: Charles Scribner's Sons, 2003), 219.

74. Hemingway, "The Killers," in *The Complete Short Stories of Ernest Hemingway* (New York: Charles Scribner's Sons, 2003), 221.

75. Hemingway, "The Killers," in *The Complete Short Stories of Ernest Hemingway* (New York: Charles Scribner's Sons, 2003), 222.

76. Hemingway, "The Killers," in *The Complete Short Stories of Ernest Hemingway* (New York: Charles Scribner's Sons, 2003), 216.

77. Hemingway, "The Killers," in *The Complete Short Stories of Ernest Hemingway* (New York: Charles Scribner's Sons, 2003), 219.

78. "Plimpton: Interview with Hemingway," in *Hemingway and His Critics*, ed. Carlos Baker (New York: Hill and Wang, 1961), 35.

79. Hemingway, "The Killers," in *The Complete Short Stories of Ernest Hemingway* (New York: Charles Scribner's Sons, 2003), 216.

80. Ernest Hemingway, "Hills Like White Elephants," in *The Complete Short Stories of Ernest Hemingway* (New York: Charles Scribner's Sons, 2003), 212.

81. Ilya Ehrenburg, "The World Weighs a Writer's Influence: USSR," *Saturday Review* July 29, 1961.

82. "Monologue to the Maestro," in *By-Line: Ernest Hemingway,* ed. William White (New York: Charles Scribner's Sons, 1967), 190.

83. Hemingway to F. Scott Fitzgerald, May 28, 1934, in *Hemingway: Selected Letters, 1917–1961*, ed. Carlos Baker (New York: Charles Scribner's Sons, 1981), 407.

84. Hemingway to Arnold Gingrich, April 3, 1933, in *Hemingway: Selected Letters, 1917–1961*, ed. Carlos Baker (New York: Charles Scribner's Sons, 1981), 385.

85. Hemingway, "Hills Like White Elephants," in *The Complete Short Stories of Ernest Hemingway* (New York: Charles Scribner's Sons, 2003), 214.

86. Hemingway, "The Killers," in *The Complete Short Stories of Ernest Hemingway* (New York: Charles Scribner's Sons, 2003), 215.

87. Hemingway, "The Killers," in *The Complete Short Stories of Ernest Hemingway* (New York: Charles Scribner's Sons, 2003), 218.

88. Hemingway, "The Killers," in *The Complete Short Stories of Ernest Hemingway* (New York: Charles Scribner's Sons, 2003), 218.

89. Hemingway, "The Killers," in *The Complete Short Stories of Ernest Hemingway* (New York: Charles Scribner's Sons, 2003), 215.

90. Hemingway, "The Killers," in *The Complete Short Stories of Ernest Hemingway* (New York: Charles Scribner's Sons, 2003), 221.

91. Hemingway, "The Killers," in *The Complete Short Stories of Ernest Hemingway* (New York: Charles Scribner's Sons, 2003), 220.

92. Hemingway, "The Killers," in *The Complete Short Stories of Ernest Hemingway* (New York: Charles Scribner's Sons, 2003), 222.

93. Hemingway, "The Killers," in *The Complete Short Stories of Ernest Hemingway* (New York: Charles Scribner's Sons, 2003), 221.

94. Hemingway, "The Killers," in *The Complete Short Stories of Ernest Hemingway* (New York: Charles Scribner's Sons, 2003), 215.

95. Hemingway, "The Killers," in *The Complete Short Stories of Ernest Hemingway* (New York: Charles Scribner's Sons, 2003), 217, 218, 220.

96. Ernest Hemingway, "A Clean, Well-Lighted Place," in *The Complete Short Stories of Ernest Hemingway* (New York: Charles Scribner's Sons, 2003), 289.

97. Ernest Hemingway, "The Short Happy Life of Francis Macomber," in *The Complete Short Stories of Ernest Hemingway* (New York: Charles Scribner's Sons, 2003), 28.

98. Hemingway, "Hills Like White Elephants," in *The Complete Short Stories of Ernest Hemingway* (New York: Charles Scribner's Sons, 2003), 212.

99. Hemingway, *Green Hills of Africa* (New York: Charles Scribner's Sons, 2003), 193.

100. Hemingway, *A Moveable Feast* (New York: Bantam Books, 1979), 13.

101. Ernest Hemingway, "On Writing," in *The Nick Adams Stories* (New York: Charles Scribner's Sons, 2003), 239.

102. Ernest Hemingway, "Big Two-Hearted River: Part II," in *The Complete Short Stories of Ernest Hemingway* (New York: Charles Scribner's Sons, 2003), 177.

103. Ernest Hemingway, *A Farewell to Arms* (New York: Charles Scribner's Sons, 1995), 165.

104. Hemingway to Dr. C. E. Hemingway, March 20, 1925, in *Ernest Hemingway: Selected Letters, 1917–1961,* ed. Carlos Baker (New York: Charles Scribner's Sons, 1981), 153.

105. Hemingway to Gertrude Stein and Alice B. Toklas, August 15, 1924, in *Ernest Hemingway: Selected Letters, 1917–1961*, ed. Carlos Baker (New York: Charles Scribner's Sons, 1981), 122.

106. Hemingway, *The Sun Also Rises* (New York: Charles Scribner's Sons, 1970), 14.

107. Hemingway, "My Old Man," in *The Complete Short Stories of Ernest Hemingway* (New York: Charles Scribner's Sons 2003), 157.

108. Hemingway to John Dos Passos, March 26, 1932, in *Ernest Hemingway: Selected Letters, 1917–1961*, ed. Carlos Baker (New York: Charles Scribner's Sons, 1981), 355.

109. Hemingway, *Death in the Afternoon* (New York: Charles Scribner's Sons, 2003), 20.

110. Hemingway, *The Sun Also Rises* (New York: Charles Scribner's Sons, 1970), 22.

111. Hemingway, "The Short Happy Life of Francis Macomber," in *The Complete Short Stories of Ernest Hemingway* (New York: Charles Scribner's Sons, 2003), 6.

112. Hemingway, "The Short Happy Life of Francis Macomber," in *The Complete Short Stories of Ernest Hemingway* (New York: Charles Scribner's Sons, 2003), 6.

113. Hemingway to Charles Scribner, October 4, 1949, in *Ernest Hemingway: Selected Letters, 1917–1961,* ed. Carlos Baker (New York: Charles Scribner's Sons, 1981), 678.

114. Hemingway to Maxwell Perkins, August 26, 1940, in *Ernest Hemingway: Selected Letters, 1917–1961*, ed. Carlos Baker (New York: Charles Scribner's Sons, 1981), 515.

115. Hemingway to Maxwell Perkins, August 26, 1940, in *Ernest Hemingway: Selected Letters, 1917–1961*, ed. Carlos Baker (New York: Charles Scribner's Sons, 1981), 514.

116. Hemingway to Dr. C. E. Hemingway, March 20, 1925, in *Ernest Hemingway: Selected Letters, 1917–1961*, ed. Carlos Baker (New York: Charles Scribner's Sons, 1981), 153.

117. Hemingway to John Dos Passos, December 17, 1935, in *Ernest Hemingway: Selected Letters, 1917–1961*, ed. Carlos Baker (New York: Charles Scribner's Sons, 1981), 427.

118. *By-Line: Ernest Hemingway,* ed. William White (New York: Charles Scribner's Sons, 1967), 188.

119. "Plimpton: Interview with Hemingway," in *Hemingway and His Critics,* ed. Carlos Baker (New York: Hill and Wang, 1961), 25.

120. Ernest Hemingway, "The Snows of Kilimanjaro," in *The Complete Short Stories of Ernest Hemingway* (New York: Charles Scribner's Sons, 2003), 50.

121. Hemingway, "The Snows of Kilimanjaro," in *The Complete Short Stories of Ernest Hemingway* (New York: Charles Scribner's Sons, 2003), 52.

122. Hemingway, "The Snows of Kilimanjaro," in *The Complete Short Stories of Ernest Hemingway* (New York: Charles Scribner's Sons, 2003), 43.

123. Ernest Hemingway, "An Alpine Idyll," in *The Complete Short Stories of Ernest Hemingway* (New York: Charles Scribner's Sons, 2003), 265.

124. Ernest Hemingway, "A Simple Enquiry," in *The Complete Short Stories of Ernest Hemingway* (New York: Charles Scribner's Sons, 2003), 251.

125. Hemingway, *The Sun Also Rises* (New York: Charles Scribner's Sons, 1970), 3.

126. Lynn, *Hemingway* (New York: Simon and Schuster, 1987), 415–416.

Index

About the Author

R. Andrew Wilson, PhD is Assistant Professor of English and Director of Writing at Cedar Crest College in Allentown, PA, where he teaches American literature, nonfiction writing, and film studies. In addition to Hemingway, he has published scholarship on authors such as Henry James and Herman Melville. When not writing or teaching, he can be found kayaking Class V rivers, hiking southwestern deserts, or climbing northeastern mountains.